# AUSTRALIA
## The First
## Five Years

by
Haydn Davis

Old Bakehouse Publications

Abertillery

First published in November 2012

ISBN 978-1-905967-42-1

Published in the U.K. by
Old Bakehouse Publications
Church Street,
Abertillery, Gwent NP13 1EA
Telephone: 01495 212600  Fax: 01495 216222
Email: theoldbakeprint@btconnect.com
www: oldbakehouseprint.co.uk

Made and printed in the UK
by J.R. Davies (Printers) Ltd.

British Library Cataloguing in Publication Data: a catalogue
record for this book is available from the British Library.

# Australia - the First Five Years

## *Introduction*

**Gondwanaland:** a name probably unfamiliar to many because it is cloaked in the mists of pre-history. Modern scientific and geological research has led to theories that, untold millions of years ago, all the continents on Earth were joined together in one gigantic land mass. It is said that about 80 million years ago tectonic movement created continental drift and the mass began to break up and separate. The vast southern portion, given the name Gondwanaland, contained within its bulk all the lands which today comprise the Southern Hemisphere. In the further disintegration that followed, Australia began its separate existence.

The dinosaurs had yet to appear (and disappear) and it would be tens of millions of years before the first human footprint was impressed in Australian soil.

After crossing in some fashion from South-East Asia, the original aboriginal natives put in an appearance a mere 50,000 years before the intrepid merchant adventurers learned the way to traverse the great oceans. And, eventually, they too found Australia...............

## *Dedication*

On May 18th 1787, two small British warships slipped their moorings in Portsmouth Harbour and sailed out into the English Channel at the beginning of what was to prove to be one of the epic voyages of British maritime history. Following them, in close order, were nine other ships, all civilian merchantmen, carrying marines, convicts and supplies. This, the First Fleet as it became known, carried a total of about 1,500 souls who were to spend the next 8 months crossing 16,000 miles of tempestuous, mostly uncharted, ocean - a feat of unprecedented and incredible navigation, discipline and human endurance!

But, if conquering this challenge were not enough, these pioneers now found themselves marooned on a pinprick of a vast, unexplored land, apparently forsaken by an uncaring home government. Years of intense hardship and suffering followed as the small colony struggled to withstand famine, starvation, disease and native attack until Australia stood on its own, safe from the claims of all other nations.

This book therefore is dedicated to the Royal Navy and especially to the officers and men of those two, tiny 18th Century warships, Sirius and Supply.

# Australia – The First Five Years

## Chapter I

### *Discovery*

That a vast, uncharted continent existed in the great southern ocean was never doubted by the ancient mariners who traded in the Spice Islands (present-day Indonesia). Even Marco Polo, centuries before them, reported hearing stories of it from Chinese travellers!

Landfalls seem not to have been infrequent by Europeans in the 17th century, although a certain French navigator, Captain Paulmyer, believed that in 1503 he was blown well off course in the Indian Ocean on to an immense coastline stretching endlessly from north to south. The first documented landings were in 1606 by the Dutchmen Jansz and Hartog on the extreme north of Cape York. Others were to follow although it is doubtful if any of them were ever aware in their lifetimes of the momentous nature of their landings.

| | | |
|---|---|---|
| 1606 | Jansz & Hartog | Gulf of Carpentaria |
| 1616 | Hartog | Western Australia |
| 1619 | De Houtman | Western Australia |
| 1623 | Carstenz | Arnhemland |
| 1627 | Thijssen | Great Australian Bight |
| 1642 | Tasman | Van Diemans Land |
| 1644 | Tasman | Arnhemland |
| 1688 | Dampier | North West Australia |
| 1697 | Dampier | North West Australia |

So many Dutch navigators had become familiar with the Australian coast that their charts now referred to the continent as New Holland!

However, after the voyages of the English buccaneer-turned-explorer, William Dampier, it was almost as if the great land mass had sunk beneath the waves. For the next 70 years or so, the courses steered by European adventurers failed to find it, although in many cases it was just over the horizon! In actual fact, no serious attempts were made, probably because all the reports which the maritime nations had received were of a bleak, uninviting aspect, oppressive heat, stinging flies, barren soil from which no fruit grew, and naked, prehistoric 'Indians' who had nothing to trade and wanted nothing but to attack any sailor landing to seek water.

Then came the memorable first expedition of Captain James Cook, the prime object of which was to carry out astronomical surveys in the crystal-clear night skies of the Pacific. When this work was concluded, he had the Crown's blessing to pursue further terrestrial discoveries, in particular that of the elusive sub-continent. This, when achieved a few months later, was almost accidental.

On March 31st 1770, having completely charted the coast of New Zealand, Captain Cook turned his ship, Endeavour, homewards. Using Tasman's charts, he steered westwards towards Van Diemans Land with the intention of proving once and for all that it was an island. It was here that fate took a hand in the form of severe southerly gales that drove the Endeavour far enough north for its first sighting of land to be the promontory that would one day be known as Cape Everard in the State of Victoria. This was on April 19th.

Excitedly charting the coast of this great land for the first time, Captain Cook sailed northwards. Like every other of the world's map-makers, he was still unsure that Van Diemen's Land (Tasmania) was not an island but a large projection firmly fixed to the Australian mainland.

On April 29th 1770, the Endeavour was steered into a large, pleasant bay where it came to anchor. Captain Cook took a pinnace away to the shore.

Magnanimously, when the boat grounded, Cook allowed his wife's cousin, the young midshipman (later admiral) Isaac Smith, to be the first Englishman officially recorded as setting foot on Australian soil.

The name given by Cook to this grand, natural basin was 'Stingray Harbour' after the number of these fish seen basking in the shallows. Not long afterwards the name was changed to Botany Bay out of respect for the thousands of specimens of flora and fauna, unknown to the western world, sketched and catalogued there.

Relations with the natives were sometimes friendly and sometimes fraught. Right from the start, the Aborigines showed little surprise at the sudden descent among them of the giant canoes sailing under white clouds, and the alien creatures encased in all manner of coloured materials that disguised the fact to the natives that they were human beings! On several occasions individual sailors were ordered to strip naked to show that they were no different, and this evoked bursts of merriment and loud cheers from the aborigines, especially the females who, like their men, spent their whole lives without a stitch on!

It seemed as if the white men were tolerated as long as they gave the impression of only being on a flying visit, but when it became apparent that this was not so, opinions changed. The aborigines showed their disapproval in a variety of ways, not least of all by putting a spear through the back of any sailor who ventured alone into the bush! Even so, the expedition's overall opinion of them was not half so bad as that of William Dampier three quarters of a century earlier when he wrote:-

'........ the miserablest people in the world........ they differ but little from brutes. They have great heads, round foreheads and their eyelids are always half closed against the flies so they cannot see far.........of a very unpleasing prospect.'

According to his journals, Captain Cook found Botany Bay to have many pleasing features, not only in its immense interest to his scientists but also for its sandy beaches, water supply and safe, sheltered anchorage. Sir Joseph Banks, the famous naturalist who accompanied the expedition, was in full agreement and spared no pains to spread the word when he got back to England. He was, after all, for many years to come, one of the few experts who had ever seen Australia.

Years later, the next visitors were not so enamoured of Botany Bay and by their actions ensured that it did not become the site of the first settlement!

When the expedition's scientists and draughtsmen felt that Botany Bay had little more to offer, the Endeavour sailed northwards and only a few miles into the voyage the opening into another bay was observed. Captain Cook did not stop to investigate but he marked it on his charts as Port Jackson and so left Sydney Harbour for someone else to discover!

The whole of the eastern coast was eventually charted and, on the way, Endeavour was nearly lost when speared by a jagged coral outcrop on the Great Barrier Reef. Fortunately the snapped-off spur of coral plugged the hole long enough for the ship to be beached and repaired.

Proceeding onwards, the Endeavour rounded Cape York at 10 degrees latitude into the Torres Strait and the sea lanes well defined by earlier Dutch, Spanish and Portuguese adventurers. Australia now had a north, east and west coast but still the great southern outline along the Great Bight showed a blank except for a vague bump in the south-east that was intended to represent Van Dieman's Land - the Bass Strait still unknown!

Before taking leave of the new land, Cook had one last rite to perform. Landing on a tiny islet off Cape York which was given the name of Possession Island, Cook, together with the naturalists Joseph Banks and Daniel Solander, raised the British flag and claimed 'New South Wales' in the name of King George III.

At that time, the new addition to the British Empire included the whole eastern half of the continent, although only the tiny enclave of Botany Bay had been explored. The great hinterland was a complete mystery and many believed that it may have surrounded a vast inland sea. It was given its name because of Captain Cook's likening what he had seen to the terrain of 'old' South Wales, an opinion which the few Welshmen on the expedition would more than likely have treated with some degree of scepticism!

## Chapter 2

### *The Bloody Code*

For years after 1770, much of the interest in Australia seems to have lapsed. Certainly no other nation showed any special enthusiasm about visiting, and any landings that were made were only for the purposes of repairs, watering ship or the stretching of legs. It would be over a quarter of a century later, during the Napoleonic Wars, before it became apparent that French ships were charting the south coast, and it was the ominous fact that French names were being given to various capes and bays that spurred the British into the eventual, urgent rush to flood Van Diemen's Land with penal settlements.

Trading did not enter into it, as word had long got about that the inhabitants had nothing to trade, and were still naked, stone-age savages. In 10,000 years they had not learned any form of animal or agricultural husbandry and were still the only people in the world who had not discovered the bow and arrow! As far as the British government was concerned, the place was a barren, hostile land, too far away, very expensive to visit and therefore completely unprofitable. A series of loosely connected events were to change this attitude in a matter of a few years.

For most of the 18th century, Britain had kept a low profile in the Indian and South Pacific Oceans, its maritime activities having almost exclusively been confined to the Atlantic. However, while Dutch and Portuguese influence was waning, the ambitions of an age-old enemy were stirring in those far-flung regions. The French were on the move!

It occurred to slowly awakening government ministers that a possible answer lay on a limitless coastline where a chain of military and naval bases could dominate a large part of the Southern Hemisphere. Should this come about, the pundits argued, and should British naval squadrons be present in strength so far from home, how could they possibly be serviced in terms of rigging, cordage and canvas when none were naturally available?

Ships required immense amounts of quality hardwood for spars and mastage: massive, straight, whole pine trees by the thousand. Flax was used by the ton to make the acres of canvas carried by the Royal Navy and merchant fleets. Both of these commodities were traditionally imported from Russia through the Baltic and were, therefore, at risk in any confrontation between France or Holland, both of whom had naval bases along the line of supply.

This problem jogged memories of a discovery made by Captain Cook on his third voyage in 1774: a remote and tiny island, 1,000 miles out in the Pacific from Australia's eastern coast. Named by Cook, Norfolk Island, the description given of this pinprick was not encouraging, but aside from its near unscaleable cliffs and lack of a harbour, there was mention of healthy flax and towering pine trees growing in profusion. New Zealand too was noted for its quality flax. Thus the argument was further fuelled for the settlement of New South Wales. A penal colony still did not feature anywhere in the government's plans but pressures were building imperceptibly and relentlessly in that direction!

Up until 1774 the American colonies had been used as a giant open prison in which to deposit the thousands of convicted criminals spewed out annually by a hidebound, cruel and heartless judicial system.

Known as 'The Bloody Code', the law of the land contained over 200 crimes for which the death penalty was prescribed. This, the most respected legal system in the world at that time, was based upon two of the most backward of concepts. The first of these was crude and basic.

It was felt that the easiest crimes to commit, being the most numerous, could only be controlled by the severest of penalties, so that the stealing of a handkerchief was equated with murder! Prostitution, strangely enough, was not a criminal offence!

Secondly, in a country where purpose-built prisons were practically unknown outside of the Capital, the mere idea of the enormous expense of building and maintaining them was too appalling to contemplate. Besides, it was not the job of the State to give free board and lodging to those whose crimes had arisen from deprivation and destitution! The same line of thinking was applied to any call for a professional police force. Only the harshest of punishments was felt to be the answer.

In circumstances where, in order to eke out even the most miserable of existences, it was estimated that at least 50% of the population courted death, it was not surprising that the lawful taking of a life became so commonplace that whole communities would turn out to watch and convert the occasion into that of a fair! The highlight of the day would be the slow choking to death of the purloiner of a string of sausages as he 'danced in the sheriff's picture frame!' Then his putrefying corpse would swing in chains at a nearby crossroads for months afterwards.

Where the offence was one of the major capital crimes such as treason, rape or murder, the hanged victim would be cut down 'before the vital spark had flown' and, whilst still conscious, disembowelled, his entrails falling out into an oil-filled dish to be burned before his eyes as they flickered their last! The corpse would then be cut into quarters, often by the local butcher who received a small fee for this duty, and paraded in a cart. The head was impaled on a spike over an archway or a bridge where it remained as a warning to to all other would-be delinquents. Grim sights like these, around which children innocently played, became no more a deterrent than the village pump! And all the time that the ogling crowds jostled each other in order to obtain a better view of the 'drop', their pockets were being picked by the dozens of light-fingered dips for whom such exhibitions were encouraging rather than intimidating!

It is a fact, however, that in the latter half of the 18th century a large proportion of death sentences were never carried out. This was not due to any sense of compassion but to an attractive alternative not only guaranteed to rid the country of its lowlife but to make a handsome profit for its financially embarrassed government.

For most of the 17th and early 18th centuries it was the custom to transport convicted criminals to the American colonies where they worked on settlers' plantations for no wages, the most basic of diets and the vilest of living conditions. They were no better than slaves!

Later they became 'bondsmen' and, after sentencing, were handed over to contractors who sold the right to their labours to American farmers and planters who were expected to pay the one way only, Atlantic crossing. To many of these transportees the system was a blessing in disguise for it removed them from a life of squalor and degradation to a reasonably well-fed, healthy environment in which, if they worked hard and found fair minded masters, they could eventually be released into a world where they could become free labourers or even self-employed smallholders in their own right. All this ended with the start of the War of American Independence and, after Britain recognised the United States of America in 1783, the victorious colonial government flatly refused to continue to be the scrapheap for Britain's misfits. Bona-fide freemen were very welcome as settlers, but not the filth dredged up from the depths of English slums. In any case, cheap white labour was being rapidly superseded by black slave labour from Africa. This at once posed the greatest of problems for the British Government: what to do with the continuing flow of law breakers churned out by the Bloody Code up and down the land!

There were few buildings suitable for the incarceration of large numbers and the enormous expense of building new ones was out of the question for a nation bankrupted by years of war. The immediate answer was an increase in the use of the 'hulks' to give breathing space in which to seek a more permanent solution.

The hulks were old wooden battleships-of-the-line - some captured French - decommissioned, dismasted and anchored in rivers and estuaries of the south of England. Woolwich, Deptford, Portsmouth and Plymouth were the main situations. For many years their purpose had been to house short sentence convicts and as halfway houses for those awaiting transportation to the Americas. Crowded they had always been but the short stays of their occupants had always ensured their manageability.

These not over-large, pot-bellied, rat-infested vessels, slowly rotting away for lack of attention, now became packed with up to 600 criminals at a time! They lived in unbelievable filth and stench, in spaces designed for 80 to 100 crew members. Many of the worst offenders were kept chained below the waterline where they never saw the light of day and breathed only the foul stink from the bilges! The remainder spent up to 16 hours a day, waist deep in the river mud, dredging silted-up channels by hand and bucket.

Their conditions were so terrible that many of the poor wretches did not survive to see the end of their sentences. A large proportion was already ill on arrival and then it was left to malnutrition, overwork or diseases such as typhus, cholera or smallpox to finish them off! There were also those whose weakened hearts ceased to beat whilst receiving excessive flogging at the hands of sadistic overseers, or else who died later from blood-poisoning when their horribly shredded backs became infected!

If a body survived all this, he still had to cope with the corruption of crooked contractors who supplied poor quality, contaminated food, not to mention coldly calculating guards who kept much back to sell for their own profit. They even lost the bulk of their belongings and clothes to fellow prisoners who brutalised all newcomers! The servers of seven year, fourteen year and life sentences had become so debauched, closely confined with other men sleeping three or four to a bunk that no depravity was beyond exercise by them. In fact, it is said that few new arrivals, male, female, adult or child, escaped the act of rape!

There had been numerous abortive meetings since the American war ended. Many committees had deliberated at the highest level on the various options. The method was never in doubt - it had to be transportation - but the vexed question was to where?

Botany Bay was not even in the running at first, mainly because by 18th century logic a prison on the other side of the world, involving the carriage of thousands of human cattle for months on end, across two mighty oceans, might just as well have been on the moon!

Several West African destinations were discussed but investigation revealed that they were such wretched, sterile, fever-ridden places that it would amount to a certain death sentence to be transported there. This did not wholly concern some of the officials conducting the enquiry as long as the problem of the hulks was solved. Fortunately, this was a minority attitude.

So Botany Bay it was, and apart from its great distance from the motherland, it appeared to possess all the attributes for sustaining a reasonable standard of life - that is if Captain Cook's enthusiastic account of 16 years earlier was to be believed! No other Englishman had been there since to check!

The idea of a mass colonisation of New South Wales was never entertained. This was purely an exercise in dumping convicts, to be continued if the initial experiment proved successful. Those who finished their sentences and obtained their release would be free to make what they could of their lives, the rest of which had to be spent in Australia. Only a rarely granted free pardon gave the right to a return home. Should a goodly proportion of time-served exiles show a propensity for reformation and a spirit of enterprise, the small settlement might even prosper. This would be a special bonus for an otherwise indifferent government, but hopes were not high of a class generally regarded as lost souls wandering in a limbo from which return was impossible.

More often than not, cases that would have been right for redemption finally emerged from the pit as violent and depraved as the worst of them! In the vicious fight for survival, erstwhile gentlemen became thugs and rapists, and ladies of gentle upbringing were turned into foul-mouthed whores. Almost all contracted venereal disease!

Here and there however, among the ostriches who sat on the committees, a few heads were disinterred from the sand and other theories were advanced of the benefits which might accrue from cultivating this wild and primitive land as a valuable member of the British Empire.

It was for instance suggested that a settlement in such a climate would enable the growth of tea, coffee, sugar cane, cotton and tobacco, giving independence from trading for these items with China, South America and the United States. It would occupy a vital, strategic position in times of war with Spain, Holland or France, and the local produce of hardwood and flax would be a key feature in the servicing of the fleet.

By 1786 the hulks were bursting at the seams with over 6,000 convicts, and the situation boiled over in a series of riots which resulted in much bloodshed and loss of life when the muskets and bayonets of the military were called into action.

In indecent haste a plan was patched together. There was little time for preparation and so it was that a makeshift operation of forced migration began, leading against all expectations to the paving of the way to the creation of the largest single country in the Southern Hemisphere!

# Chapter 3

## *The First Fleet*

In August 1786, the Cabinet approved a proposal put forward by Viscount Thomas Townsend Sydney, the Home and Colonial Secretary, and his under-secretary, Evan Nepean.

In choosing a leader for their expedition they looked no further than the semi-retired list of Royal Navy officers, and gave Captain Arthur Phillip his commission as 'Governor of the Territory of New South Wales.' Here was a man, currently a gentleman farmer, who had given over 30 years of competent but unspectacular sailoring to his country; his record as a navigator was unimpeachable. Now, in early middle age, he was being given the opportunity to remove his name from the anonymity of the Navy List and place it in the hall of fame!

By October 1786 a fleet of 11 ships was assembled. This was the largest group of vessels, with the largest passenger list, sailing the longest voyage ever undertaken in poorly charted seas using the primitive navigational techniques of the day! Many of those involved in the final organisation did not believe that the scheme could succeed, at least not without great loss. With others the attitude was that of good riddance!

The First Fleet consisted of the following ships:-

| | | |
|---|---|---|
| Royal Navy | Sirius | Flagship |
| | Supply | Tender |
| Merchantmen | | |
| Store ships | Borrowdale | |
| | Fishburn | |
| | Golden Grove | |
| Convict transports | Alexander | |
| | Charlotte | |
| | Friendship | |
| | Lady Penrhyn | |
| | Prince of Wales | |
| | Scarborough | |

None of these ships, preparing for a journey of nearly 16,000 miles, was any bigger than the ferries that ply across modern Sydney Harbour!

All through the winter of 1786 the fleet was fitting out in various south coast harbours and, not unexpectedly, suffering from a series of footling delays! Overzealous bureaucracy and cheese-paring bargaining with contractors caused postponement time after time. Captain Phillip kept up a constant bombardment of letters in terms both pleading and angry, to the Admiralty, Home Office, War Office, Foreign Office, Board of Trade and the Privy Council but all to no avail! He was almost convinced that in these circumstances he could easily lose half of his charges before the journey's end and thus reduce his own reputation to ruins.

The convicts did not all go on board at the same time which meant that the unlucky first arrivals spent the rest of the winter chained below decks in accordance with the directive that prisoners should not be unshackled and given deck exercise until well out to sea. The plight of these poor wretches was dreadful: no daylight, no fresh air and chained four or five to a shelf under a deck head giving only 4 feet 6 inches of headroom!

Victualling and provisioning continued in a haphazard manner as weeks were wasted through mismanagement, mislaid or lost documentation and even plundering along the way! At the final reckoning, when sailing could be put off no longer, Captain Phillip was appalled to discover that in spite of all his badgering the success of the whole operation was seriously jeopardised by grossly inadequate under-funding and furnishing. The lack of enthusiasm of government ministers and the penny-pinching of their departments, combined with the employment of unscrupulous sub-contractors, had ensured shortages in all sorts of vital supplies.

Worst of all, the fleet eventually sailed without the dossiers of the majority of the convicts and there is no record that they ever turned up. Thereafter, nobody in authority knew for sure the crimes for which their prisoners had been convicted, or in many cases the length of their sentences!

When the women convicts arrived, it was noted that their previous long incarceration in the hulks had resulted in the reduction of their clothes to verminous rags, and many of them were near-naked! Little thought had been given to stocking up on the coarsest or cheapest cloth with which to tide them over their first year in exile.

The food supply left very much to be desired. The salted beef was old - some of it had been in storage for years - the flour was considerably short measured and made up with substandard rice. No scorbutic food was included although, since Captain Cook's voyages, the cause and treatment of scurvy was well known. Rather than a voyage half way round the world, quantities seemed as if calculated for a crossing to the Americas!

Tools of all description were of shoddy construction and delivered in numbers much reduced from those ordered. Hammers, nails, saws and adzes for the carpenters, hoes, spades and forks for the gardeners and farmers, would all have to be shared on a rota system. Not one plough was sent out with the First Fleet and it took seven more years for the first to arrive!

The same slipshod planning appears to have gone into the selection of convicts with trades that would have been the most useful, indeed vital, to early building operations. There was only one experienced builder, one farm labourer, one fisherman and a few carpenters; the rest were a nondescript bunch who had only ever been used to doing as they were told and possessed callings that would not be required for years to come i.e. bookbinders, clerks, gentlemen's servants etc.

On the whole, the women formed a similar example. What, for instance, on a wild shore, could be expected of dressmakers, milliners, glove makers, housekeepers and parlour maids? Among all of these, only one very well represented profession was likely to be in great demand and it was the oldest!

By far the largest group among both sexes was that containing the real dyed-in-the-wool villains: those who were born to thieving, who did not know what it was to do a day's honest work and had no inclination to find out!

The whole sordid, confused enterprise was ready after a fashion in early March 1787. The eleven ships assembled just outside Portsmouth, six of them stuffed with human cargoes suffering the indignities of the damned!

Nearly 1500 persons embarked.

Between 736 and 772 (reports vary) were convicts.

There were three times as many males as females.

A dozen or so were children.

The youngest boy was a nine-year-old chimney sweep sentenced to 7 years for stealing clothes.

The youngest girl, aged 13, had stolen a hat and a gown.

The oldest convict was a woman rag-and-bone dealer aged 82 sentenced to seven years for perjury. She also became the colony's first suicide when, within a few months of landing, confused and abandoned, she hung herself from a gum tree!

Nationality-wise, the bulk of the convicts were English followed by Scots and Irish. There were only four Welshmen on the prison decks of the First Fleet - a pattern repeated throughout the history of transportation. Few present-day Australians can claim convicts among their Welsh forebears.

None of the first batch had been found guilty of major crimes although there had been some degree of violence in acts of robbery.

The remainder of the party was made up of Captain Arthur Phillip and his nine administrative staff, four companies of marines numbering 247 officers and enlisted men, 27 marine wives, 19 children and 443 seamen.

No voluntary settlers were included and this was because the enterprise was charged with unknown risks and was a most unattractive proposition to anyone with a rosy prospect in mind. It was still only an experiment in removing the great blemish that shamed the nation to a mysterious, far-off wilderness to be conveniently forgotten. Colonisation, other than penal, was the dream of a few government advisors, men of some vision whose counsel was promptly rejected by purblind parliaments.

In the chill, dark, early hours of May 13th 1787, the 11 small ships weighed anchor and slipped out into the English Channel. Quietly and unobtrusively began what in time would be seen as one of the greatest phases in British, and ultimately, Australian history. For all the wrong reasons the last great nation to be discovered on Earth would arise out of an incredible display of seamanship and   the endurance of unspeakable hardships by the 160,000 or so rejects from British society who were eventually forced to make the journey!

The first leg of the marathon voyage was uneventful and was carried out in fairly moderate weather. It was, however, the convicts' first introduction to the motion of ships at sea and just as they were becoming adjusted to the abominable conditions in which they were held, the new curse of sea sickness descended upon them! Stomachs which at the best of times had little to give were torn almost inside out by the constant, pitiful retching. At exercise times the upper deck was as extensively spattered with bloody puke as the rags that the prisoners wore and the all-pervading stink clung to the ropes and canvas despite the purging by the heavily salted sea air!

Into these slippery, slimy surroundings the ships' officers and marines could rarely bring themselves to venture. Most of their time was spent behind the heavy timber and metal-spiked walls which were a feature of all convict transports, thrown up right across the ship just forward of the poop deck to protect the guardians from being rushed in the event of a riot. The ordinary sailors fared much worse in that they had to range far and wide in the normal course of their duties and this only strengthened their resolve to pile on the convicts' miseries!

But if conditions out in the open were so atrocious, those in the convicts' quarters were almost impossible to imagine and they had to be borne during the long periods of night confinement and often in the daylight hours when the weather turned bad.

None of the ships of the First Fleet had been designed to carry human cargoes, much less in the numbers now demanded of them. The quarters consigned to them were those dark, airless areas in the lowest depths where the headroom could be as little as 4 feet 6 inches! Into these spaces the convicts were packed, chained together in fours and lying on plank shelves with little bedding and hardly the room to stretch a muscle. In these fetid surroundings the effects of the mal-de-mer were very much more pronounced and were made even more insufferable by the menace that lurked only a few inches beneath where the filth-encrusted bodies lay.

Even in the best kept of ships the bilges were not renowned for their fragrance! The lowest cavities, just above the keel, were the receptacle for much of the liquid leakages from above which carried down with them all sorts of nautical refuse and scraps of food; rats swarmed here! This stale, stagnant magma possessed peculiar effluvia that every sailor learned to live with, but which were highly obnoxious to the uninitiated. It was no wonder therefore that with a few hundred extra sets of sickly bowels evacuating into too few overflowing buckets, more alien substances should invade the bilges!

There was always movement in this viscous broth and even on the calmest of days the slopping sound underfoot was ever-present. When, however, the fleet's sails were full-bellied with propitious winds livening up the swells and breaking the tops into whitecaps of hissing foam, there was a different tale to tell!

As the little ships nosed into these rollers, rising at steep angles to burst through the crests and then dropping sharply into the troughs, the sudden savage jolt as the downward movement was arrested caused the flooded bilges to slosh furiously in all directions. Powerful jets of the contents spurted continuously between the poor deck planks, drenching the convicts in a horrible mélange of the original bilge swill liberally laced with mucus, vomit, rat droppings, urine and faeces, both diarrhoeal and dysenteric! Open sores, ulcerated limbs and the flayed backs of the recently flogged did not profit from such embrocation!

When the weather moderated or indeed on those occasions when the fleet lay almost becalmed, the respite for the prisoners was little less unbearable. The air in the stink holes in which they rotted by night became a suffocating fug which echoed to the moans and groans of the sorely afflicted, to the animal-like cries of those who were rapidly becoming deranged and the croaking gasps from a hundred throats straining in vain for a breath of untainted air!

Amidst this nightmarish wretchedness there was one feature that seemed to be at odds with physical deterioration.

Male and female convicts were separated by specially built, reinforced bulkheads which soon proved no match for the determination of those whose sexual needs seemed proof against any amount of privation. Ships' logs regularly recorded floggings of men caught in women's bunks and of many of the whores who persistently sought the men's company. More often than not the sailors and the marines spent nights among the women whose services were easily acquired for a noggin of rum. When the hatches were opened each morning some of the women were too drunk to climb out, whilst others, badly hung-over, rushed to the rails!

One of the fleet's surgeons wrote in his diary: *'Nightly, in the convict's quarters, they rutted like stoats!'*

Under such a primitive regime, the basis of which was a total indifference to suffering, it is remarkable that so many of the original convict assignment reached the final destination alive. The records show that during the eight months at sea only 48 died of the 1,500 persons who embarked in England - and eight of these were not convicts!

The route taken by the First Fleet was the longest possible (nearly 16,000 miles), but it was also the one where the prevailing winds and tides gave the most assistance. On June 3rd, three weeks to the day after leaving Portsmouth, anchors plunged into the blue water of Santa Cruz harbour at Tenerife in the Canary Isles.

A week passed during which water stocks were replenished and some meat and fresh fruit taken on board. The Spanish governor lavishly entertained Captain Phillip and his officers whilst the ships' crews and marines found their own pleasure in fiery Spanish brandy and the bagnios of the red light district! The convicts remained battened down in the steaming lower hulls where relaxed vigilance left them free to pursue their abandoned practices without fear of the lash!

On June 10th the voyage was resumed.

Sailing southwards, the Cape Verde Islands were skirted on the 18th and the fleet drove onwards into the Atlantic Narrows and the Doldrums where windless days slowed progress. Deep in the tropics, the convicts were let out for longer periods but on returning below they found conditions more hellish than ever! The intense heat turned the lower decks into ovens and caused every biting, gnawing, stinging creature to emerge from the bilges and every other crack or crevice! Rats by the hundred became entirely fearless and fleas by the million invaded the rags and straw in which the prisoners lay!

No one was spared. The bugs were no respecters of rank or class, and convicts and captors suffered alike - It was particularly disagreeable for the better bred marine wives and children! While the fumes of boiling tar laboured to suppress the plague, it was all too apparent that new miseries would soon be visited on the convicts for their totally unpremeditated part in its introduction.

The convoy ploughed steadily on south-westwards, the least cumbersome of the ships circling round from time to time to chivvy along those that straggled like errant sheep. At night they kept station by keen observation of each other's flickering masthead lamps and the firing of cannon. It is a tribute to their officers' seamanship, in particular that of Captain Phillip, that there were few occasions in these boundless, watery wastes when any ship was out of sight of one or another of its companions!

June stretched into July.

During the periods of slack winds and slow progress in the equatorial regions, a precautionary reduction was made in food and water rations but suddenly the little armada was picked up by the bustling south-easterlies and bowled merrily onwards. Parallel to their course now was the coast of Brazil, as yet unseen but confirmed by the increasing number of seabirds that screeched and scavenged in the ships' wakes.

On August 5th 1787, the 64th day after the last landfall in the Canary Islands, the ships of the First Fleet found safe haven in the harbour of Rio de Janeiro, over 6,000 miles from their homeland but still considerably less than half way to Botany Bay.

The Portuguese were well disposed towards the British, especially the Governor of Rio with whom Captain Phillip had made previous agreeable acquaintance. There was to be no more sea time for a month whilst serious stocktaking and running repairs were carried out. It was here that Captain Phillip hoped to make up some of the glaring shortfall in provisions created by ham-fistedness back in London. The other priority was the replacement of split sails, broken rigging and the recaulking of hulls and decking which had been sprung by their battering at sea.

Some effort was made to clean the ships, but as the convicts were not allowed above deck, little headway was made in their quarters. The sick list was extensive but the surgeons and their assistants could not give the attention they would have liked because the moment they ventured below and entered the realm of filth, boils, ulcers, vermin and, above all, the indescribable stench, stomachs rebelled and threw up!

There was however some little satisfaction for the women convicts, many of whom had been reduced to almost total nakedness. Some had been in this state since leaving the hulks! The rags of many had rotted on their backs but a large number of the weaker women had been bullied out of theirs by the fierce, hard-faced cows who had once paraded their wares in disreputable, inner city streets! Ever conscious of this shameful state of affairs for which he had no budget, Captain Phillip found a partial solution in the purchase of lengths of cheap, rough material and stores wrapped in jute sacking which could be converted into simple chemises.

For those who could go ashore, there was pleasant sojourn despite the heat and the flies because, even in those days, Rio was a colourful, warm-hearted place. The convicts, however, spent the whole month locked away beneath decks that alternately scorched in the hot Brazilian sun or steamed furiously following short-lived torrents of tropical rain. As bad as their voyage had so far been, they all longed for anchors to be weighed so that they would once more see the sky and be washed by clean, salty spray.

The moment arrived none too soon on September 3rd, and later that day the shoreline of South America had receded into a low, dark blur on the western horizon as the Tropic of Capricorn was crossed.

It was not necessary to drop much lower into the South Atlantic. Cape Town was 3,000 miles away but no more than six degrees latitudinally. It required but a short beat south-eastwards to catch the sou-westerly winds and be driven in gently curving course towards the Cape. This time, the crossing, being more direct and unbeset by any navigational or weather problems was made fairly quickly - five weeks for such a distance by 18th century standards was very reasonable.

Discontent and boredom became decidedly marked among the gaolers who had nothing better to do than gamble, trail fishing lines and take pot shots with their muskets at seabirds or porpoises. Their rum supply had almost run out and to replace it in Rio they had bought a supply of cheap, nasty but very potent Brazilian spirit called 'aguardiente'. Under the almost lethal influence of this firewater, marines and seamen lost all inhibitions. Little irritations became big squabbles which often turned into vicious fights. Officers were abused and in their turn became abusers also. Somehow the drink reached the prisoners (mostly through the women) and it became commonplace in the lower decks to hear ringing cheers and the clanking applause of chains as bodies rolled about kicking and clawing at each other!

Loss of deck exercise and increasing weight of leg-irons were common forms of punishment but the usual was flogging, and it was almost a daily ritual for the bosun, wielding his dreadful cat-o-nine-tails to shred the backs of several convicts with the customary 25 to 50 lashes. In a few extreme cases, the more ungovernable women were similarly dealt with, stripped to the waist and spread-eagled against the mast. The 10 lashes that they normally received were cleverly laid on by the expert flagellant so that the purple wheals never actually broke the skin, but the brutish curses brought down on their tormentors by these women outmatched anything that the men could produce!

Marines and crew members were not excluded from such punishment - indeed they were likely to suffer more as examples were made and at least one lieutenant found himself hugging the mast for drunken insubordination and fighting with a brother officer! Cape Town on October 13th 1787 could not have been more welcome!

Another month was spent here savouring the last feel, sight and smell of European civilisation; there would be no other chance to take on supplies that could be of value in the unknown life ahead.

The Dutch colony was not so accommodating to the British. A precarious peace had existed between the two nations for a hundred years but memories were long and old grudges died hard. The Cape Towners were in no mind to be generous to a British fleet making an incursion into oceans that Holland's navigators, traders and colonisers regarded as their own. Captain Phillip found that he had to bargain hard for every concession. There were no discounts and it was not above the skinflint Dutch merchants to get rid of second-rate goods that had cluttered their shelves for years!

If the officers, marines and sailors hated the place for its heat, flies and lack of hospitality, the convicts at least, sweltering in the darkness below, received some small benefit from a more nutritious diet of the fresh meat and vegetables that Phillip insisted were necessary if the remaining journey were to be endured. However, it was a case of swings and roundabouts for the convicts. With the possible exception of seed for planting and essential food supplies, much of the cargo was extremely bulky and little extra provision had been made for it. The convicts, cramped as they were, had to move over to make room for more than 500 farm animals which included 2 bulls, 3 cows, 3 horses, 44 sheep, 32 pigs and a grand assortment of poultry. The animal feed alone required substantial space. More clothing and miscellaneous equipment were obtained but still nobody thought of a plough!

When all was securely tucked away, made fast and battened down, the third, final and most challenging leg of the voyage began. On November 12th, the eleven ships made the quick turn round the Cape of Good Hope and dipped south-east-by-east into the virtually unknown and most forbidding waters ever sailed by man. Their course once again took the form of a shallow curve that carried them into the Roaring Forties where, over 6,000 miles ahead, it would pass under Van Diemen's Land (still believed to be joined on the Australian mainland) before the final swing north to Botany Bay.

The first part of the journey followed a route well known to Dutch traders who used the powerful westerlys to carry them to the Amsterdam and St. Paul Islands, half way across the great southern Indian Ocean. Here they found new winds to take them north to the Spice Islands, giving the western Australian coast a wide berth. At this point, however, the First Fleet had to keep straight on into waters where only two men - Abel Tasman and James Cook - were known to have sailed before!

This part of the ocean comprised the longest stretch on the Earth's surface unimpeded by any land mass that would slow down and break up the fierce westerly winds for which the region was noted. For long periods the little ships were subjected to the weather's fury. Under ominously dark, madly scudding cloud cover, sails reefed to the minimum, they clawed their way up the velvety green backs of enormous ocean rollers, crashing through walls of blinding foam at the crests, then hurtling down the other sides until brought up with the mighty jar that heralded a new ascent!

It was at moments like these that masts and spars were most at risk from the dangerous 'whip', but these plucky vessels led charmed lives. Day and night the pumps were manned, for all were leaking, but otherwise there was no major damage. As could be expected, below decks all was chaos! Every few minutes, several tons of ice-cold water thundered across the decks, down the hatches and smashed through the helpless convicts. Marine Lieutenant Clark, the scribe on board 'Friendship', recorded that: *'a great deal of water went below decks, washing marines and convict women from their beds and separating lovers ......!'*

Conditions were as hellish as in any previous phase of the voyage but now there was the added anguish of the animals which became very distressed and filled the air with pitiful cries as they were half-drowned and hurled about their pens! Many died of shock!

The south coast of Van Diemen's Land was sighted after eight weeks, and by January 10th 1788 the fleet had made the turn northwards. On January 18th, Captain Arthur Phillip, on board Supply, (he had transferred from the labouring Sirius) sailed between the heads of Botany Bay and dropped anchor. In the next 36 hours the rest of the ships limped in.

Thus ended what must qualify as the greatest voyage in the history of British shipping. For any one ship to make such a journey and lose, say, 10% of its crew would not have been surprising, but for 11 vessels carrying 1,500 souls to sail for 8 months, sustain only 48 fatalities and all arrive together was little short of miraculous!

The credit of course belonged to a 50 year-old, little or no account naval officer, brought out of retirement and commanded to do his country's dirtiest job. The moment that he set foot in Botany Bay, Arthur Phillip became first Governor of New South Wales - in effect of the whole continent as it was then known - with full power of government and a mandate to develop the country in the true image of the Mother Country

# Australia – The First Five Years

## Chapter 4

### *Settling in - Early setbacks*

First impressions of Botany Bay as a place to set up shop were not inspiring and only a day or so of exploration confirmed in Phillip's mind that it was most definitely unsatisfactory!

Confidently expecting to find signs of the attributes which Captain Cook's log had mentioned in such glowing terms (and which Sir Joseph Banks, back in London was still extolling), the pioneers looked in vain. Here was no safe anchorage or gardener's paradise! The inadequate depth of water in the bay and its numerous sandbars made it ill-suited for berthing ships, except near the entrance where there was much less protection from the Pacific winds and rollers which created a permanent swell.

Cook's 'green, open meadows' were non-existent and the soil was poor, sandy or marshy where it did not have to be cleared of thick walls of matted grasses, scrub and dense woods of green eucalypt and red gum that stretched as far as the eye could see. Even the water supply was poor; the solitary, shallow stream that had watered the Endeavour seemed to be the only one for miles. Before any serious investigation began, a working party of marines and seamen went ashore to cut forage and green grass for the surviving sickly animals.

In the course of these preliminary excursions, first contact was made with the natives, who showed belligerence by shouting angrily and making threatening gestures with spears and clubs. They had not been overly intimidated by the sudden appearance of the strange, white creatures; those who had been fishing from bark canoes in the bay showed remarkably little concern when the giant wooden castles under canvas clouds sailed among them!

A few hours after landing, Phillip's men were making better progress in their relations. Gifts of coloured ribbon and beads soothed away tensions and soon the primitive were mingling freely with the civilised on the beach. Communication could only be by complicated signals.

The aborigines' main confusion seemed to be over the white men's clothing. They themselves were always seen to be completely naked, both males and females, except for bone or shell adornment and body painting. Having never seen any other kind of human being, they were not even sure what their visitors were! They seemed to think that their clothes were their skins and they pulled and pinched perplexedly at the red uniforms of the marines and the blue of the naval personnel. The raising of a cocked hat from an officer's head caused gasps of amazement!

Besides the nature of these peculiar white creatures, there was also uncertainty about their sex, so in order to settle aboriginal doubts, Lieutenant Gidley King ordered one of the marines to expose himself! A little uncertain at first, the man unbuttoned his white breeches and then, grinning at his comrades, he brazenly relieved himself in the sand! A short, stunned silence was followed by roars of approval and much banging of spears on shields. The females, who had not up till then shown themselves, emerged from the bush and added shrill giggling to the applause!

Trouble between natives and newcomers had to be avoided at all costs. This was the brief given to Captain Phillip in his Royal Commission as Governor:-

'........ they must not be molested or wantonly destroyed. Anyone giving them unnecessary interruption in the exercise of their several occupations must be brought to punishment according to the degree of the offence. Relations with them must be in amity and kindness. You must conciliate their affection.'

This was how Australia's native population was originally intended to be treated. History, however, has revealed the dreadful course that the future of the aboriginal race was to take at the hands of the genocidal white man. A ruthless form of racial prejudice was to eventually produce massacres, cruelty, imported diseases and deprivation of their hunting grounds. In 1788 there were estimated to be 500 tribes comprising over 300,000 aborigines. In 1876, the last full-blood died in Tasmania and by the middle of the 20th century only 45,000 remained in the whole continent. A conscious-stricken government then introduced measures to preserve the race and it now stands at a more respectable 165,000.

It took but 24 hours for the Governor to make up his mind about Botany Bay. At 6am on January 21st, he and Captain Hunter, commander of the Sirius and surveyor to the fleet, left in three longboats rigged with sails, through the Botany Bay Heads and proceeded northwards.

They had covered no more than 12 miles when another gap appeared in the rugged coastline and, steering into it, the explorers found a harbour the like of which they had never before seen! This was the Port Jackson of Captain Cook, named by him but not felt to be worth even a cursory inspection as he charted his way up the coast.

A few miles inside, Governor Phillip spied several sandy coves on the south shore, the largest of which he selected as being an ideal site for his settlement. Everything about it seemed auspicious especially its potential as a port, sheltered position, good fresh water stream and the great depth of water in the outer roadstead where, Phillip wrote:- 'A thousand sail of the line may ride in the most perfect security in the finest harbour in the world!'

As the party penetrated further, it encountered large groups of natives lining the banks of the various creeks, shaking their spears while chanting what sounded like 'Warra, warra, warra!' Translation was impossible but it was quite obvious by the demeanour of the tribesmen that 'Welcome' was the last thing intended!

It took three days for the investigation to be completed but on the 24th the three longboats were back at Botany Bay and orders were being given for the fleet to sail again.

That morning, as anchors were about to be weighed, there came a surprising interruption as two unidentified ships were seen far out to sea. Phillip decided to postpone sailing, but only for one day. It had already occurred to him that these new arrivals might be a French expedition that was known to be in the Pacific. Early next morning (the 25th), in the midst of a tremendous thunder storm, Phillip took Supply out through the Heads with great difficulty against adverse winds and tides. The other ten ships found the task too dangerous so decided to follow when the storm abated. At first light on the 26th, the hurricane (for that was how Surgeon Arthur Smyth, on the Lady Penrhyn described it), died down and the fleet again weighed anchor.

At this precise moment the two strange ships appeared in the entrance to the bay and must have received some shock at the sight of the fleet leaving what appeared to be so attractive a haven. Captain Hunter on Sirius dallied long enough to exchange signals and greetings when the vessels revealed themselves to be 'La Boussole' and 'L' Astrolabe' commanded by the French explorer Francois de la Perouse, now into the third year of a voyage of discovery.

This was the last ever seen of the French expedition, for it disappeared mysteriously and traces of its wreckage took 30 years to turn up on Pacific island shores!

Meanwhile, in Port Jackson, the Governor had gone ashore from Supply, taking with him his officers and marines. The Union Flag was run up and four toasts were drunk, to King George III and other members of the Royal family. The ceremony ended with a volley from the muskets of the marine guard of honour, answered by the boom of Supply's cannon. January 26th has been celebrated ever since as Australia Day.

Having cleared the troublesome Heads of Botany Bay, the other ten ships headed by Sirius found themselves at 4 pm entering Port Jackson and by 6 pm were all safely anchored near Supply. Governor Phillip christened the place Sydney Cove after Viscount Sydney, the man responsible for their presence there. Today this is the bustling waterside area of the vast city of Sydney known as Circular Quay and if one looks closely at the paving nearest to the water, the broken rambling of the of the original 1776 shoreline is to be seen delineated by brass studs.

The formal task of colonising began early on the following morning. The male convicts were ferried ashore and formed into work parties. They had not stood on solid ground for the best part of twelve months, so their sea legs, combined with atrophied muscles, caused many a collapse in the soft sand and rotting forest floor! What is more, they were being called upon to carry out physical labour-something that many had forgotten all about and which most had avoided all their lives!

It was a filthy, struggling rabble that the officers and marines had to organise and distribute to the various tasks. It was not made any easier by the fact that no one possessed any particular skills to make use of. Field kitchens and feeding schedules had to be arranged, the skivers and malingerers had to be sorted out

Arthur Philip, Captain Royal Navy, Commander of the First Fleet, 1st Governor of New South Wales 1788-1792. Born 1738, died 1814. Retired 1805 with the rank of Rear Admiral.

*Wikipedia*

Prison hulk 'Discovery' on the Thames at Deptford. This ship accompanied Captain Cook on his last voyage. Painting by Edward W. Cooke 1811-1888.

*Courtesy of the National Library of Australia*

Prison hulk at Portsmouth (prisoners embarking). Painting by Edward W.
Cooke 1811-1888.

*Courtesy of the National Library of Australia*

Prisoners from the hulks at Woolwich working on shore. Published by Bowles & Carver.

*Courtesy of the National Library of Australia*

HMS Sirius. Built in 1780 as 'The Berwick', for the East India Trade. She was badly burned in a fire and was bought and rebuilt by the Royal Navy in 1786 and renamed 'Sirius'. After her arrival in Part Jackson, she remained as a supply ship and sailed to the Cape of Good Hope in October 1788 to obtain food supplies for the starving colony. After returning she was wrecked off Norfolk Island on the 14th April 1790. She was 540 tons and skippered by Captain John Hunter, a future governor of New South Wales.

*By courtesy of the State Library of New South Wales*

HMS Supply, the smallest of the Fleet, being only 170 tons and 70 feet long. Carrying 50 people and skippered by Captain Henry Bull, she led the fleet most of the way, primarily because of her speed. Little is known of the brig's early history, but it seems that she was built in America in 1759 and was commissioned by the Admiralty in October 1786. The Supply returned to England where she was renamed 'The Thomas & Nancy'. It seems that she carried coal on the Thames until around 1806.

*Courtesy of the National Library of Australia*

Entrance to Port Jackson (Sydney Harbour) close under the South Head. This would have been the way the First Fleet would have seen it in its first sighting. Painted by George Raper, First Fleet artist 1769-1796.

*Courtesy of the National Library of Australia*

The First Fleet in Sydney Cove 17th January 1788. Painted by John Allcot 1888-1973.

*Courtesy of the National Library of Australia*

from the genuinely ill on the huge sick list, heavy punishment irons had to be struck off before many could move - and all under a relentless Australian summer sun which took temperatures into the high 90s, despite sporadic bursts of thundery rain.

Those first few days were days of cursing, kicking, rifle-butting and beatings with switches cut from the undergrowth as the marines vented spleen with undisguised pleasure. In the bush, out of sight of officers, they were most malicious to those whom they believed had robbed them of their military dignity and reduced them to the role of common jailors! However, within a remarkably short time, chaos became improved to manageable disorder as the first steps were taken in the building of a nation!

The diary of Marine Captain Watkin Tench gives an eye-witness account of the return to some semblance of system:-

*' In one place a party cutting down the woods; a second setting up a blacksmith's forge; a third dragging a load of stones or provisions; here an officer pitching his marquee, with a detachment of troops parading on one side of him and a cook's fire on the other ...... '*

The difficulties were enormous and the labour to overcome them very hard, even for strong, fit men let alone men whose muscles were wasted from emaciation and long disuse. Tree clearing almost from the water's edge proved the poor quality of the tools, and grubbing the stumps from the hard, gritty soil took its toll in hernias and near-broken backs! One ship's scribe noted how it took twelve men nearly five days to grub out one tree!

There were no draught animals - no horses or oxen - only ragged wretches chain-harnessed into yokes. Most of the encouragement was given by a fair bit of buffeting. The really vicious treatment of convicts did not make its appearance until some years later under governors who were pressurised by a home government to make the sentences of convicts as unbearable as possible. Some deluded legislators in London held the notion that the denizens of the foulest slums in England were deliberately committing crimes so as to obtain transportation to what they believed was an environment a fraction less ugly than they were already used to!

At the end of the first week, enough ground had been cleared around the shore of Sydney Cove for an encampment. So far, everyone, gaolers and prisoners alike, had slept in the open, lying on the bare earth, scratching and slapping at the myriads of tiny bugs and spiders that covered them. Canvas was to be their main shelter and a tented village gradually took shape, with the Governor's marquee set well away to one side as befitted his rank.

It took nearly a fortnight longer to erect enough tents for the women's compound, and it was not until February 6th that they were allowed to disembark. Most of that day was spent in transfers from ship to shore.

As evening approached, one of the violent, New South Wales summer storms broke, bringing with it powerful squalls that ripped open and blew away many of the tents. The ground became one huge quagmire. In the ensuing free-for-all there was no question of supervision or the maintenance of discipline. The marines were as desperately pressed by the extreme conditions as the rest and in any case were only concerned with the prevention of escapes. What the convicts did to each other within their confinement areas was the least of their gaolers' worries that night!

So it was that the male prisoners broke out of their enclosures, raided the liquor stores, drank themselves silly and pursued the females. Rum soaked sailors from the ships came ashore to join in the fun. There must have been something like 600 men trying to share less than 200 women! Floundering about in the spongy earth, splashing, laughing, cursing bodies fell upon each other in a gigantic orgy of abandonment. The homosexuals among them - and they were not in short supply - celebrated the fact that for a few short hours they could with impunity commit their sodomite acts for which, in those days, the penalty was death!

When the sun rose next morning the scene was one almost of devastation in the wake of the great tempest and the brutish carnality that had accompanied it. It is doubtful if any woman, other than the old or the sick, had that night escaped rape, some several times over! Those who had resisted suffered severe beatings into the bargain! The only consolation, if it could possibly be described as such, was that many of the women, being prostitutes anyway, made willing partners!

Those girls whose crimes were of a gentler nature, who had never experienced the filthy squalor of the city stews and who had that night been violated time and time again, must have felt that they had descended into the lowest regions of Hell!

Governor Phillip was outraged!

In the morning, when he received news of the affair, when he saw for himself the state of the mud-bespattered, badly hung-over convicts as they dragged themselves from the ooze where they had fallen exhausted, and when he heard the sorry weeping of the injured women, his fury knew no bounds! He could not, however, take action until the main event of the day was concluded.

By mid-morning on that 7th day of February 1788, all the convicts were seated on the ground, encircled by their marine guards with muskets and fixed bayonets; all sailors who were off watch were present also. Governor Phillip, standing before a dozen or so of the senior officials who were to form the first colonial government, listened as his judge-advocate read the terms contained in two sealed documents on the table before him.

About 1,400 witnesses listened impassively as the Commission of King George III for the founding of the colony of New South Wales was followed by Arthur Phillip's commission as First Governor of the territory, an area prescribed as extending from Cape York in the extreme north to the southern coast of Van Diemen's Land and westward as far as longitude 135 degrees - half only of the modern continent. The other half, with only parts of its coasts charted, was then still known as New Holland. Van Diemen's Land was still believed to be attached to the mainland. The commission also stated Phillip's almost omnipotent authority in all matters of state legislature and especially his power of life or death in relations to his 'subjects'. By this declaration, the colony became official.

If, at the end of the speechmaking, the convicts were expecting a perfunctory dismissal, they were sadly mistaken!

Governor Phillip now stepped forward and, in a way completely alien to his character, exploded in a tirade of invective directed at the convicts for their behaviour during the previous night. First came the accusations of their shameful depravity (most likely accepted by the convicts as is water off a duck's back), and then the threats!

If any of those who stood before him felt in future the inclination to repeat these exploits, punishment would be of the severest, even to the shooting on the spot of any man found in a woman's tent, or hanging if rape were proved after the event! The convicts were left in no doubt as to other crimes for which necks could be stretched. Chief among these was the thieving of livestock or the limited foodstuffs landed from the ships and meant to last until a few seasons gave self-sufficiency.

The chastisement continued for some time and ended with the ominous warning that those who did not pull their weight would not be fed! It was something of a shock for the work-shy convicts to discover that their only salvation now lay in years of the hardest graft!

Phillip was as good as his word, and it was only a matter of three weeks before the first death penalties began to be handed out. The first legal hanging in Sydney Cove was that of a lad, barely 17 years old, who had stolen some salt pork and dried peas. On his way up the gallows steps he cried for his mother and God's forgiveness!

The Governor was not a harsh man; many of his underlings thought him too soft for a job demanding the exercise of fierce discipline. But then, their Lordships in London had not chosen him principally for such tendencies but for his brilliant navigational skills.

He could well have demonstrated his right to reprieve the poor youngster on grounds of his tender age but, much as it must have plagued his conscience, he realised that it would not be in his best interests to show such a weakening of resolve. A strong example had to be made. Why, however, he commuted the death sentences on two older men for the same offence, committed at the same time, is open to question! They each received 300 lashes and were chained to two others for six months!

The formula appears to have had its required effect and it is remarkable that in a population consisting chiefly of thugs, murderers, rapists, pimps and prostitutes, only eleven male convicts were executed in the next four years. In the fifth year the number was seven but six of these were soldiers of the New South Wales Regiment!

When it came to punishment of the drunken lechers of February 6th, many of them received brutal flogging on the 'triangles'. These were timber structures

35

where the victim's hands were drawn to the apex high above his head and the feet were bound wide apart at the base. For a time there were not enough to satisfy the demand and forest trees were fitted with the necessary fetters. Fifty to a hundred lashes from the wicked cat-o-nine-tails were normal and the marine floggers delighted in making each sentence as painful as possible. They had several ways of achieving this and each of them lent his own personality to his performance. One could caress a back for up to two dozen lashes, raising only angry weals; whenever he pleased he could split the weals into bloody gashes. Another would time the strokes, leaving an interminable 30 seconds of anguish between each one!

It was not unknown, where the lashes were well above the average i.e. 300, for the sentence to be carried out in two stages with several days intervening. After the first 150 lashes the prisoner would be cut down. A week later he would be brought back to the triangle and the newly formed scabs of the first flogging would be torn away by the second! It should be remembered that using the 'cat' meant that, in a hundred lashes, 900 knotted flails would lacerate the flesh! There was no retreat around the cove where the hiss and crack of the whips could not be heard!

Towards the ends of the busier sessions, eye-witnesses vowed that the clearing where the triangles stood became a bloody quagmire in which the floggers squelched as they moved about. At night the place was alive with small bush animals and swarms of blood-sucking insects that came to enjoy a gory feast!

Elsewhere, those who had been the day's guests at the triangles lay on their stomachs, biting on pieces of stick, groaning the night away as their agony denied them sleep.

Among the more hardened, obstinate and totally ignorant convicts were some who were determined not to give their tormentors the satisfaction of fully appreciating their suffering. They gritted their teeth and flinched with every stroke but uttered not one sound. This ploy only had the effect of making the frustrated floggers lay it on extra hard in order to extract some show of emotion. Increased injury was the only result of this ineffectual show of defiance!

Surprisingly, few in Sydney died from this barbarous punishment; it was years later that many were cut down lifeless in the hell camps of Norfolk Island and Van Dieman's Land following the ridiculously excessive numbers of lashes meted out by sadistic camp commanders. It is on record that one man managed to survive for seven days after receiving 700 lashes! Well into the 20th century there were elderly Australians who could remember having seen the ancient, badly healed, disfiguring whorls and scars on the backs of grandfathers and great grandfathers.

Women did not figure on the triangles to any great extent but when they did, it was usually because they had needled their way through a long series of offences, the most common of which was fighting with each other. One group especially noted for this had earned for itself the name 'The Fighting Five' and were reputed to be 'the five worst whores in Christendom'. The other criminal nuisance in which the women excelled was verbal abuse and everyone at some time or another came in for their share. Some of the sneering, sarcastic asides spoken deliberately within earshot of the guards were allowed to ride, but others, particularly slurs on wives or parentage, meant a spell chained to a tree on a diet of bread and water, or else partial immobilisation in heavy irons.

A much less painless penalty, but nevertheless felt to be the most humiliating, was the shaving of the guilty women's heads, and this was carried out to the accompaniment of violent struggling and terrible cursing and screaming. Many hands were required to hold down the filthy, half-naked bodies as the last vestige of their vanity, teeming with lice and nits, was taken from them!

It was these foul-mouthed products of the gutter who persistently heckled the gaolers, got involved repeatedly in hysterical affrays and who dared the threat of the ball and chain once too often - they were the ones who went to the triangles cursing on the way, cursing all through their ten to twenty-five lashes and cursing all the way back to their hovels! Their performances were regarded as grand entertainment by the watching male convicts who delighted in howling a count-down with every stroke of the cat!

This then was the material with which Governor Phillip was expected to claim and consolidate another piece of the Earth's surface for the British Empire. When the real need was for honest, hard-working settlers, Phillip had something like 700 bone-idle, thieving ruffians, devoid of any basic skills, whose brains seemed to be permanently concentrated in their loins. They were incorrigible recidivists, malaise incurable and all but a minority condemned by their own actions to live forever in the twilight world of the unredeemable. Their stain was indelible. So, the thieving, fornicating, fighting and flogging went on!

When the First Fleet arrived, it brought with it the makings of a colonial government. Under sealed orders was the commission of the future constitution and instructions as to its operation. Some of the men whose task it was to put these orders into practice were named and the Governor was empowered to elect others as he saw fit.

A brief list of the more notable characters who travelled with the First Fleet is as follows:-

<u>Arthur Phillip</u> *Captain Royal Navy. First Governor of New South Wales 1788-1792. Named Manly Cove in honour of the 'dignified' stature of the Aborigine tribe that he found there. Speared by one of them through the shoulder and back in August 1790 and survived after being rowed for several hours back to Sydney Cove. Retired because of ill health and the effects of his wound but resumed naval duty and finished his service with the rank of Admiral.*

<u>John Hunter</u> *Captain Royal Navy. Commander of HMS Sirius until it was wrecked on Norfolk Island in March 1790. Expert surveyor and cartographer. Second Governor of New South Wales 1795-1800.*

<u>Philip Gidley King</u> *Lieutenant Royal Navy. Aide-de-camp to Governor Philip. Third Governor of New South Wales 1800-1806.*

David Collins   *Lieutenant Royal Marines. The colony's Judge-Advocate although having no legal training. Promoted Deputy Governor in 1806.*

Robert Ross   *Major Royal Marines. Commanding officer of the Royal Marine garrison and deputy governor to Phillip with whom he was constantly at odds. Aggressive and completely unco-operative.*

John Shea and James Campbell   *Captains Royal Marines. Joint deputies to Major Ross.*

George Johnston   *Lieutenant Royal Marines. Twenty years later, with the rank of major, he led the coup that deposed Governor William Bligh (of Bounty fame).*

Watkin Tench   *Captain Royal Marines. One of the many scribes who kept records of the First Fleet's voyage and its aftermath. Captain Phillip encouraged as many people as possible to keep written records - at least one to each ship. Tench was the most observant, the most literate and certainly the most prolific.*

John White   *Surgeon-in-Chief and scribe.*

William Balmain   *Assistant surgeon.*

Denis Considen        *- ditto -*

Thomas Arndell        *- ditto -*

Altogether there were eleven doctors with the fleet, but only those above remained in the colony. That they brought 97 per cent of their charges through to Australia under the most atrocious conditions, was evidence enough of their dedication and skill. Their splinting repaired numerous broken bones and prevented not a few amputations; their coarse stitching closed many an ugly, open wound and even their primitive nostrums, elixirs and poultices had measurable effect in the treatment of fevers!

Reverend Richard Johnson   Described as *'hardworking but a querulous bore'*, he administered to the colony's religious needs. Conducted 21 marriage ceremonies in the first two weeks after the colony's founding, but to his eternal regret after that, legal unions seemed to go out of fashion! No matter how he tried, he had little success in the conversion of the convicts so that he eventually became as bitter towards them as their gaolers. Badly disillusioned, he returned to England in 1800.

Augustus Alt   *Surveyor-General.* His one claim to fame seems to have been the preparation of a plan to develop Sydney Cove as a capital city worthy of New South Wales. He envisaged a main street 200 feet wide for the little village! Needless to say, little more was heard of him or his plan after that.

First and foremost in the foundation of what was hoped to be a prosperous colony, was the need to care for the health and welfare of the first citizens who were to build it, be they convicts or freemen. Therefore it was in the best interests of everyone to agree that the watchword must be self sufficiency. The clearance of good soil by hundreds of willing hands, the speedy sowing and germination of the seed followed by a rich harvest, would supply fresh food and enough new seed for the year after. Such was the theory that, in practice, went seriously wrong!

The soil around Sydney Cove proved to be shallow and poor. Digging down just a few inches everywhere uncovered layers of sandstone. Drainage was bad and root systems could not develop. The single freshwater stream that ran into the cove was not copious enough to provide irrigation - in fact it did not have the power to drive a small waterwheel! Earthen tanks were dug into its banks to form small reservoirs and to give greater depth for the sinking of buckets, hence its name: the 'Tank Stream' now culverted beneath the streets of modern Sydney.

The seed brought with the fleet was heavily contaminated with weevils; much of what was left failed to germinate.

If all this were not bad enough, the poor quality of the tools now became all too apparent and proved that they were not up to the extremely heavy usage required of them. While the axe blades blunted easily on the unusually hard wood of the gums, and the helves snapped from hoes, pick-axes, spades and adzes, much of the livestock was stolen by the aborigines or wandered into the bush of its own accord never to be seen again!

The disinclination of the convicts to put their backs into it and the outright refusal of the troops to undertake anything but garrison duties, gave added impetus to the settlement's downward slide into a situation of famine!

The food brought out from England was now over a year old. The salt pork and beef was rotten and full of maggots but nevertheless continued to be eaten. It was sometimes supplemented by kangaroo meat but this was unpalatable to the settlers and in any case powder for their muskets was in short supply. Fish appeared on the menu only occasionally for the very good reason that only one skilled fisherman could be found among the convicts!

In all these respects they were at a distinct disadvantage to the aborigines who were good hunters whose health did not appear to suffer from a diet that caused British stomachs to turn over. Nearly everything that moved was fair game to the black man and all the more appetising if it was found squirming under a rock! To him, snakes, lizards, worms and the most nauseating, bloated grubs were as venison! With the greatest of ease he could knock down kangaroos and a wide variety of smaller animals and birds using spear and boomerang, whereas the best the convicts could do in their weakened state was to throw badly aimed and ineffective stones.

When a native hunting party camped in the bush close to Sydney Cove, the aromas from their cooking fires nearly drove the half-starved white men mad, and the sight of the well-fed, pot-bellied tribesmen against their own gaunt, emaciated frames was hardly a stimulus towards better relations!

There were just too many mouths to feed, so Governor Phillip began to take steps to lessen them.

Before leaving London, he had received orders to colonise Norfolk Island, a tiny speck only 15 square miles in extent, discovered by Captain Cook in the Pacific Ocean, about 1,100 miles east of Port Jackson. Because of French activity in that area, the Government ordered that the British flag should be raised on the island as soon as possible. At the end of February therefore, Phillip ordered HMS Supply to the island. The plucky little, 170 ton brigantine of only seven guns, carried Lieutenant Gidley King, two of his men, six ticket-of-leave men and fifteen convicts. Their instructions were to commence building a settlement. With them they took a few livestock, seed for sowing and food for six months. This party was followed by another a few months later.

By May, the situation around the shores of Port Jackson had deteriorated very seriously. In addition to the regular high quota of sick and disabled, another 200 went down with scurvy and there was still no expectation of the edible greens which could supply the necessary vitamin C.

Some of the small islands in the grand harbour were found to have soil of much better quality than on the mainland, and on them a fair degree of horticultural success was achieved. Unfortunately, these vegetables were not safe even when protected by an expanse of water! Many disappeared during night-time forays by silent raiders in small boats!

Phillip had no way of knowing if further supplies were on the way from England. He recalled the intransigence of Their Lordships over fitting out the First Fleet; he had been appraised of the enormous cost of the expedition - it worked out at about £1,000 per convict - he was well aware that there were those at home who had been prepared to wash their hands of the whole affair as soon as the last sail sank over the horizon. Never a day went by that he did not fix his glass on the Port Jackson heads in the hope of espying the entrance of a new ship from England.

It was now time for the ships of the First Fleet to start leaving Port Jackson. All of them except HM Ships Sirius and Supply were merchantmen whose private owners had been contracted for the convict voyage. Every day that they remained so engaged was costing the Government a fortune! On the 13th May 1788 therefore, Lady Penrhyn, Charlotte and Scarborough left for Canton in China where they were to pick up cargoes of tea for the East India Company. On 13th July, Alexander, Friendship, Prince of Wales, Borrowdale, Fishburn and Golden Grove sailed for England. This left Phillip with only the two Royal Navy ships: Sirius, a second-hand merchantman previously named Berwick, converted into a poor excuse for a man-of-war, and Supply, naval tender, much newer, much more seaworthy and the fastest sailing ship in the fleet.

The Founding of Australia by Governor, Captain Arthur Philip, Sydney Cove, January 26th 1788. Painting by Algernon Talmadge.

*Courtesy of the State Library of New South Wales*

Loss of HMS Sirius off Norfolk Island, 19th March 1790. Painting by George Raper, 1769-1796.

*Courtesy of the National Library of Australia*

Norfolk Island. Rescue of the crew and provisions from the wreck of HMS Sirius. By an unknown Port Jackson artist.

*Courtesy of the National History Museum*

Governor Philip, wounded by an Aborigine spear, being rescued from Manly Beach. By an unknown Port Jackson artist.

*Courtesy of the National History Museum*

Sydney Cove 1790. By an unknown Port Jackson artist.

*Courtesy of the National History Museum, London*

Sydney Cove 1790 seen from the north shore. Today, Sydney Opera House dominates the centre of this scene. By an unknown Port Jackson artist.

*Courtesy of the National History Museum*

Circular Quay (Sydney Cove) 2008.

*Wikipedia*

Sydney Harbour, Circular Quay (Sydney Cove) top left.

*Courtesy of the Rodney Heywood.*
*Aerial photograph taken 1st February 2006.*

# Australia – The First Five Years

# Chapter 5

## *On the verge of starvation*

The urgent search for a land of plenty went on, with teams scouting ever more deeply into the wild country around Sydney Cove. In April 1788, the efforts paid off and a large area of fertile soil was discovered 15 miles to the west, made more easily accessible by way of a river that flowed into Port Jackson. Phillip named it Rose Hill after his close friend at the Treasury, Sir George Rose, although three years later, in June 1791, it was given its aboriginal name, Parramatta (Head of the Waters). A labour camp was quickly established, land cleared, furrowed with hoes and the remainder of the colony's tiny supply of seed was sown.

This, however, did not help the current situation which was rapidly reaching famine proportions! The Governor's own livestock were transferred to his Rose Hill farm and by July he had only one sheep left after the rest of his flock, his Afrikander bull, pigs and poultry wandered off. With them went a valuable source of natural manure!

Phillip realised only too well the direness of his predicament. He estimated that, severely rationed, the decaying stock of English food could last no more than twelve months, during which time they would probably die. Their only hope of salvation was the arrival of further supplies from England and/or a successful harvest of grain and greens at Rose Hill. There was sufficient doubt about both these prospects to require immediate alternative action to be taken.

Phillip took it!

First, he further cut the food ration, as always in his fair and charitable way, ensuring that everyone, no matter his station, should share equal portion.

Then he ordered Captain Hunter to sail HMS Supply to Cape Town and bring back as much food and other life preserving materials as quickly as possible. Typical of the incredible voyages in which 17th and 18th century mariners excelled this was to rank with the best of them.

Hunter's shortest route was straight back westwards across the southern Indian Ocean and return, a round trip of some 12,500 miles, but this would have been in the face of the strong westerly winds of the Roaring Forties on the outward journey. It was, in fact, much quicker to go eastwards across the South Pacific, rounding Cape Horn at the tip of South America and then to carry on across the South Atlantic to South Africa. From there on, the return trip would be the same as the First Fleet had taken. Overall it meant covering a distance in excess of 17,000 miles, and it had to be done in all haste by seamen who, at the start, were suffering the early stages of scurvy!

The Supply sailed in October 1788 and the thousand or so hungry occupiers of Sydney Cove settled down to wait!

By this time the ragged tents which had been the first accommodation for the convicts and their guards had given way to a shanty town of awful huts, no more than boxes, constructed from the trunks of cabbage palms and mimosa saplings daubed over with the red clay common to the area. The roofs were of rushes cut from the mud flats of Rushcutters Bay, and hardly constituted a covering at all. These hovels constantly had to be rebuilt after heavy rain washed away the mud plaster that held them together!

The quest for more permanent building materials was an on-going project and it was not to be all that long before the only convict with building experience, James Bloodworth, found suitable clay and was instructing others in the manufacture of primitive bricks. Moreover, along the banks of the Parramatta River, there was evidence of good building stone. Mortar could have been a problem because the vital ingredient of limestone was unavailable. The answer was found on a local beach that consisted almost entirely of clam, oyster and other mollusc shells cast there over thousands of years by the aborigines. The convict women were put to work collecting them, pulverizing them and burning them to make a suitable substitute for the undiscovered mineral.

Progress was painfully slow. Over 300 convicts could not work because of scurvy and other debilitating ailments, including serious eye trouble caused from the smoke of the burning lime. Cuts and open wounds for instance, took twice as long to heal where scurvy was present.

The rest of the meagre work force needed the closest supervision if only to obtain a minimum day's work. The marines were at their perverse and obstructive worst; backed by their leader, Major Ross, the deputy Governor, they refused all responsibility as overseers, leaving Phillip no option but to make do with 'trusties' selected from among the convicts themselves. This led to further complications because these privileged prisoners used their new powers to cover up worse thieving than that of their charges!

Then there were the aborigines!

After six months of the white man's occupation it was dawning on the native Australians that their visitors had come to stay. Their attitude changed and their indifference and passive unfriendliness of the early days turned to outright hatred and aggression as they found themselves being steadily dispossessed of camping and hunting grounds that had been theirs by right since the ancient Dream Time.

Road building crews were attacked, their members speared or clubbed to death. Labourers, cutting trees or cultivating clear areas, were felled by vicious boomerangs thrown with unerring accuracy by unseen assailants in the dense, surrounding bush. Anyone working alone was at special risk!

In the outlying labour camps the nights were made eerie and sleeping very difficult by the cries of birds and grunting of animals as the aborigines signalled to each other in their excellent mimicry. At best, on the following mornings, essential tools or stores might be missing - at worst, the battered corpses of a marine guard or a convict would be found in the fringes of the forest! Pursuit was next to useless. The black man melted into his natural environment as if magically transformed into one of the native gums.

Retributive raids were carried out, often involving the massacre of an innocent hunting party and the accompanying women and children. Such incidents were sometimes also the occasion for rape but, as yet, even the most hardened soldiers could not bring themselves to lay with bodies unwashed since birth, smothered in fish oil and stinking to high heaven!

Remaining true to the orders given to him in the King's Commission, Phillip frowned on these incursions and, while conceding that examples had to be made, he forbade the cruelty for which these measures became known.

Governor Phillip and his Judge-Advocate, David Collins, were left little room for manoeuvre, believing wholeheartedly, as they did, in justice through the process of laws developed over centuries in the Mother Country. Treating these Stone Age people as law-breakers was useless when the term had no meaning for them. In 10,000 years they had made no laws for themselves and had only ever come to know the law of survival. Among them it was even permitted to commit murder, especially of wives who were frequently speared to death in nothing more than domestic tiffs! What was the use of bringing such 'innocents' before the white man's courts of justice in order to mete out punishments for which, in their eyes, the reasons were incomprehensible?

The niceties of this argument were lost on Major Ross and his marines. They almost wrecked the whole judicial system in refusing point-blank to serve as magistrates or jury members!

They now hated everyone: Phillip for his leniency in his treatment of the convicts and his insistence on equal food rations for all, the prisoners for the same dietary reason and for being the root cause of everyone being in this god-forsaken place to begin with, and the aborigines because they were filthy, dangerous sub-humans!

The marines almost hated themselves for their own noticeable decline. Gone were the spick-and-span uniforms and tri-corn hats; heavy wear and tear was taking its toll in the fading of brilliant tunics, the staining of the once pristine white breeches and the easily torn, threadbare materials, unmended, with buttons unreplaced because of the shortage of needles and thread. New footwear could only be formed from the skins of animals after the soles fell from what had been immaculate boots. On occasions it was not unusual to see members of a military squad parading barefoot!

In such a way the long, Australian summer drew on from 1788 to 1789, the energy pumping out of the camps as the inmates sank into the lethargy of a lingering death. They snapped at each other, skirmished with the natives and at all times watched with gnawing anxiety for some sign that they were still remembered in the outside world.

In April / May 1789, something of a tragic but unsolved mystery occurred. The native tribes that occupied territory in the proximity of Port Jackson were decimated by a shocking epidemic of smallpox that spread like wildfire. Corpses of the recently dead were to be found by the dozen, lying around in the bush with the signs of the loathsome disease all too apparent. However, and here was the mystery: whilst the epidemic reached considerable proportions, it had the strangest of qualities in that it did not touch one member of the white population! This was a most unusual manifestation of smallpox and the speculation of the more upright colonists, especially the diarists, has been carried down the years to become a controversial plaything of modern day pundits.

There were those who suspected that the virus was introduced by the white man in a deliberate act of genocide intended to rid the colony of a 'nuisance!'

Watkin Tench, the most reliable of the many scribes, was in no doubt that the many doctors of the First Fleet did carry with them the means whereby such a foul deed could have been perpetrated. They were known to have in their medicine chests both syringes and bottles containing samples of the deadly scab, but this was more than likely killed by conditions of storage on the long journey from England, the length of time which had elapsed and the extremes of temperature to which it had been subjected.

Rumour was rife nevertheless, and understandably, stories were told of infected food and blankets left out for the aborigine to steal. Surely, however, if this were to have happened, such articles would have been taken by the colony's own arch-thieves, the convicts, who were desperate for food and bedding. For obvious reasons they would not have been let in on such a dreadful scheme!

Then again, in these primitive conditions, any form of quarantine was impossible so it would have been the easiest thing for any infection from the bush to enter the British camps. Those in authority, especially the medical men, would have known this and would have been the first to acknowledge that a designed act of extermination could quite as well have meant the signing of their own death warrants!

Governor Phillip was certainly not one to countenance such a deed, so firmly was he entrenched behind the idea of obeying his King's command to respect the natives. Watkin Tench dismissed the idea as 'A supposition so wild as to be unworthy of consideration'. Nevertheless, the mystery still persists. Where could the epidemic have started? Who could have introduced it? Why was it restricted only to the aborigines? If indeed it was somebody's secret, then that somebody took it to the grave!

At about the same time, an anonymous officer made the following comment in a letter to his parents:-

*'The country is beyond doubt a wretched one. There is no timber fit for naval purposes; no fibrous grass or plant from which cordage can be made; no substance which can aid or improve the labours of the manufacturer; no mineral productions; no succulent vegetables......... and, which is the most serious consideration, no likelihood that the colony will be able to support itself in grain or animal food for many years to come!'*

Back to this bleak scenario of famine, disease, violence and intense mistrust came the little brig, Supply. One day in May 1789, her topgallants were spotted far to the south by the lookout on Sydney Heads and, several hours later, her anchor was plunging to the bottom of Sydney Cove. Excited crowds gathered on the shore.

Supply's epic voyage halfway round the world to save the colony, had taken seven months and had proved entirely successful - for the time being! Survival was prolonged but not guaranteed. Without more aid from Britain the future was still precarious!

Every available inch of the ship's holds was packed with a total of 56 tons of flour and seeds of wheat and barley. The valuable cargo was boated ashore and dispersed to storage areas under marine guard. Several dozen ten-gallon ankers of rum and Dutch gin were whisked away to the officers' stores.

The rest of the year passed with little recorded incident, and drew to a close with the faintest flickering of hope. By November, 700 bushels of wheat and smaller quantities of barley and maize had been produced at Rose Hill. The first time-served convict was given an acre of land, tools and some seed. This man, James Ruse, was one of the very few with farming experience and when he had proved that he could support himself, he earned another 30 acres within two years. Ruse is looked upon as the father of Australian farming - he was certainly the first emancipated convict to become wealthy from the soil. Unfortunately, his love of drink and gambling was, one day, to take it all away from him!

It was over two years since the First Fleet had found Port Jackson and no further ships from England had followed. Still present in many minds was the conviction that the operation had been a one-off dumping of unwanted humanity. Governor Phillip himself could not believe that they had been forgotten - that the British Government had suffered a change of heart in its penal policy so soon after its inauguration!

There was no way of knowing how the tiny, two-year-old settlement on Norfolk Island had fared; at least history has not recorded a return visit by either of Sydney's two warships in the meantime. Even if Phillip had obtained such news from any other source it would have received a mention in his files, but these have never been found, and neither have any of those of any other governor up to the year 1800 - another mystery!

Once again it was time for a life or death decision. It was the courageous facing up to a succession of these dilemmas that led to a rapid run-down in Phillip's health and his ultimate retirement.

In early March 1790, he dispatched the leaky old Sirius and the smaller, much more seaworthy Supply to Norfolk Island. They took with them 221 convicts, a contingent of nine marine guards and their commanding officer, Major Ross, who was to be Lieutenant Governor of the remote settlement. This action served Phillip well in two ways: it dramatically reduced the number of mouths pecking away at the Sydney Cove food stores, and it got rid of Ross who had been a constant thorn in Phillip's side. No more would he be troubled by the marine officer's niggling opposition to practically every policy promoted in the interest of the colony's development!

Furthermore, HMS Sirius was instructed to proceed on from Norfolk Island to Canton in China to obtain more provisions. HMS Supply was to take on anything that the island could spare and return post-haste to Port Jackson.

As it proved, Norfolk Island had nothing to offer, even after two years of settlement. From the start it had been a terrible struggle in spite of the promise in its rich soil. The place was alive with rats, voracious insects and parrots which, coupled with the extremes of weather, had played havoc with the first seed sowings. There were still only fifty acres under cultivation and as a source of flax (for sailcloth) and good quality marine timber, the island was a complete failure!

On leaving to start the long haul to China, Sirius got no farther than an offshore reef where she was wrecked beyond recovery; all except one of its crew got safely ashore. The date was 19th March 1790.

In April, Supply got back to Sydney with the doleful news. For the colony it was disastrous; for the Governor a personal tragedy in the knowledge that he had lost half his remaining fleet. Now his only lifeline was one small ship and even this was withheld from him by his having to send it almost immediately to Batavia in another desperate bid for provisions.

The food situation was now so bad that further draconian cuts were seen to be necessary. In April 1790, each person's share became 4lbs of flour, 2½lbs salt pork and 1½lbs of rice per week, all in rotting condition. On these sparse amounts everyone became easily exhausted and more prone to sickness. The original half speed of the labourers and vital work in the fields came almost to a standstill!

Clothing, if it could be called that, was so crude and tattered that convict could be mistaken for guard; the women were slightly better turned out because of their natural ability to make do and mend and their dexterity in matching and patching.

On the morning of June 3rd 1790, with low cloud, stiff breeze and a chill in the air, Lieutenant Watkin Tench was sitting in his humble shack contemplating his doubtful future when: 'A confused clamour in the street drew my attention. I opened my door and saw several women with children in their arms, running to and fro with distracted looks, congratulating each other ..........I needed no more but instantly started out .........by the assistance of my pocket glass my hopes were realised. A brother officer was with me but we could not speak; we wrung each other by the hand, with eyes and hearts overflowing!'

Thus was reported the arrival of a single ship that proved to be the harbinger of the infamous Second Fleet. The long awaited sails belonged to the transport, Lady Juliana, carrying 222 women convicts and children, most of the latter having been born on the voyage!

Governor Phillip's initial feelings of profound relief turned to dismay when he realised that the ship carried only a little flour to go with all the extra consumers who, because of their puny limbs, could hardly have been expected to add muscle to the communal effort that the colony so lacked. A few days later, his fears were somewhat diluted when the Lady Julian's supply ship, Justinian, sailed in.

These ships had left England in July 1789 and had therefore taken eleven months to reach New South Wales. However, the women, all said to be *'of marriageable age'* did not seem to have suffered overmuch. Some of them, nevertheless, had undergone horrific experiences.

The lesson started early - on the first day out from Old England's shores no less. Straight away, the crew and the accompanying soldiers entered the women's quarters to make selections of partners for the long voyage ahead. The ship's master turned a blind eye!

As the convicts included sick, pregnant, plain and older women (up to age 45), there were squabbles over those who were younger and more presentable. The cattle show ended with the willing pairing-off of the majority - they were, after all, only continuing their normal street trade - and the rape of the terrified remainder who resisted the advances of the odorous and often drunken sailors. Each time one of these sessions came to an end in the certain knowledge that the experience would be a daily occurrence for months to come, these women faced a new barrage of verbal and physical abuse from the envious harridans who had been ignored! Not for nothing did the Lady Juliana become more commonly known as 'The Floating Whorehouse!'

Children were conceived and born before the voyage was over. Those women who started out as virgins (and there were a few) arrived in Australia as hardened and degenerate as any of those whose origins were in the vile rookeries of the big cities!

This was to be the pattern for most of the early transportation years. So few women were sent out in relation to men (one in six) that they were treated only as objects of sexual gratification, completely degraded, passed about under the guise of servants but used principally as prostitutes. Many of them were already of this ilk: drunken, foul-mouthed and completely uninhibited as far as their bodies were concerned. They had nothing else to bargain with in the fight to survive, and this had been the chief contributory factor in their original convictions.

Many of the time-served women of ill repute set up shop in disused huts on the western shore of Sydney Cove, an area known as The Rocks, where their numbers steadily increased over the years as concubines were thrown out by partners desirous of change! The Rocks remained Sydney's red light district throughout the 19th and early 20th centuries; it is also the support for the southern end of the harbour Bridge.

A small minority of the women, however, were of gentler upbringing, having fallen on hard times and convicted of petty thefts occasioned by the need to save themselves and their families from starvation. Indeed, there were those who were innocent of any crime but who were falsely accused by wicked masters when refused their favours! The monstrous trauma that overtook these poor creatures, caused by the unspeakable conditions into which they were suddenly pitched and the bestial company they were forced to keep, could only be borne by the most reluctant acceptance of their lot and sinking into the same slough as the rest!

This wild sexual appetite, outweighing even the constant gnawing pangs of starvation, the common regard that all women were whores, and the whole-hearted preference to make temporary partners of them instead of wives, ensured that the vast majority of the first-born Australian generation was from the wrong side of the blanket!

Even the highest ranks of the legislature were not above taking convict women as concubines, and both future governor, Philip Gidley King and Judge-Advocate David Collins sired children by three 'servants'. Major Foveaux, a future commandant of Norfolk Island, stole a convict woman, Ann Sherwin, away from one of his junior officers but he did at least marry her some years later.

After the convicts themselves, the largest share of the blame had to be taken by the transient element of the male population: the soldiers finishing their overseas tours of duty and the sailors who only stayed for the turn-around of their ships. They distributed their seed freely about the colony before returning to the arms of their loved ones in England!

Hundreds of children were to run wild in Sydney Cove and its outstations, few knowing their true fathers. They were born free but were tainted forever in the eyes of the upright by the stain of their convict mothers. Never did any nation depend so much for its foundation on such a wealth of illegitimacy!

So it was that the 220 women of the Lady Juliana and their children came ashore and were absorbed into the human tide that already lapped the Port Jackson shores. The waiting male convicts quickly forgot their disappointment over the poor replenishment of food stocks and were soon taking advantage of the fresh supply of womanhood!

At least now, the beleaguered colonists learned from the officers of the Lady Juliana that another fleet was not too far behind. They were also told why they had so nearly starved to death for want of relief from home. There had been a store ship on the way and it should have reached Sydney the previous March. The Guardian was carrying a two year supply of food but got no further than Cape Town. Off the Cape, on Christmas Eve 1789, the ship hit an ice-berg and was so badly damaged that its mission had to be abandoned!

Governor Phillip heard this news with great chagrin for it meant that it was this shipwreck that had caused him to send HMS Sirius to its doom!

Only a few more weeks were to pass before the occupiers of Sydney were to be confronted by the most dreadful scenes in the history of transportation!

# Chapter 6

## *The Second and Third Fleets*

The Second Fleet (excluding Lady Juliana and Justinian) was very different from its predecessor of over two years earlier, both in numbers and assembly. The First Fleet had been wholly government financed, albeit using privately contracted ships. It had proved very expensive and this had great bearing on the change of method,

This time, the job was fully contracted out to entrepreneurs who sub-contracted to the ships' masters. The price offered and accepted was £17-7s-6d per prisoner, and Parliament, very ineptly, promised this for each body embarked and not for those landed alive in Sydney. This made it more profitable for the rascally masters, when prisoners died en-route, to save their food rations for sale in Sydney!

The ships provided were old: Neptune the largest, Surprise the leakiest and Scarborough making her second trip. The first two had lately been used in the Afro-Caribbean slave trade and their holds were still fitted out in the heartless manner usual to the transportation of black slaves. Rows of flat, boarded bunks each took at least four bodies, side by side, in tiers of three or four, with only about two feet of headroom between each! Nobody raised the question of adaptation to more humane standards. Nor were the slave manacles replaced; they differed from the normal at the anklets where, instead of several chain links allowing limited movement, there was but a single, nine inch long bolt that cruelly locked the legs together so that even a shuffling walk was well nigh impossible. As if this were not bad enough, the ships' masters used valuable space, which rightfully should have been given to the convicts, to carry goods to be sold for profit in Australia!

By January 1790, all preparations were made and the transports fully loaded. Surprise carried 256 male convicts; Neptune had 424 male and 78 female and Scarborough 253 males. The total convict cargo was 1,011. The Second Fleet sailed on 17th January.

Despite the fact that Governor Phillip was cut off completely from his home government, he took every opportunity to keep up his pleas for more selective attention to be paid in the choice of convicts in future fleets. He still hammered away at the need for at least fifty farmers and a broad assortment of other craftsmen including builders, engineers and blacksmiths. Only three opportunities were afforded for these letters to be sent: on the First Fleet's outward voyage at Rio and Cape Town, and when Supply had gone for help in the previous year. If the letters were passed on to the appropriate addresses, they were once again ignored and the only judgement used was that of scraping the bottom of the barrel!

On this occasion, it would appear that the main aim of their lordships was to cleanse the hulks of the crippled, the sick and the demented. Hardly a completely fit person was put aboard the three transports and a fair proportion was at death's door even as they were bundled over the gang planks!

When the ships sailed, their ailing cargoes were packed closer than sardines, chained to their low shelves and destined to be battened down in the semi-darkness for most of the voyage. The reprehensible activities of the captains and crews began almost immediately; the usual violations took place among the women on Neptune and the not ungenerous food rations laid down by government order were cut to starvation level. Although making better time than its predecessor, the Second Fleet met with the same extremes of weather - frying under tropical suns, becalmed in the airless Doldrums and lifting and plunging in the Roaring Forties as the ships were driven across the great southern oceans!

Below decks, conditions were far worse than any yet described. On hot, dry days, from the open hatches, there rose a foul smelling vapour that even the burning of tar could not dissipate!

The dying commenced from Day One!

First went those who were breathing their last as they were carried aboard; following closely were those whose constitutions, much weakened by severe treatment in the hulks, were no match for chronic sea-sickness and the constant drenchings by seawater.

The sadistic captains cut the issue of food to levels whereby life was hardly sustainable and their officers made free use of the whip at the first signs of protest. The desperation to survive drove many convicts to loathsome depths. Writing of their dreadful experiences long afterwards, ex-convicts recalled how, waking up to find themselves shackled to a corpse, they had not reported it for up to a week, or until the putrefaction became unbearable, in order to make use of the dead man's food ration!

No one knew how many of these deaths may have been induced during the night - the vital spark being extinguished by furtive hands placed over the mouths of those too weak to resist! Deaths were rarely questioned; corpses were regarded as only so much animal carcase to be left with their chains as weights and tossed overboard without blessing. In the cases of convicts for whom a combination of salt water, chafing irons and rough, splintered planks brought ugly, weeping ulcers, the poultices applied by the medical assistants were often torn off and eaten!

Hardly a day passed without pathetic, human bundles dropping into the ships' wakes. They were still being put overboard from Neptune as it entered Port Jackson and the last splashed in at the mouth of Sydney Cove!

The Death Fleet, as it became known, was truly well named and the hell-ship, Neptune, appropriately so. On Surprise, 36 convicts died out of 256; on Scarborough, 73 out of 253, and on Neptune the horrific total was 158 out of 502, altogether making 267 deaths from 1,011 or just over a quarter of all convicts! To make things worse, 486 arrived who were terminally ill or too weak to work!

Surprise sailed into Sydney on 26th June 1790, Scarborough and Neptune two days later.

The crowds gathered on the west bank once more, bubbling with excitement at the prospect of new company, extra food and news from home. As the first boats approached the shore, the hubbub grew but as their contents were disclosed a stunned silence fell over all!

Most of the convicts had to be lifted out; many collapsed face down in the shallows, some in convulsions, and some never to rise again. Of those who made it on to the beach and fell to their knees to kiss the sand, there were not a few who rolled over and died on the spot! All were encrusted with filth, boils and ulcers. The few who could retain an upright stance stumbled about completely disorientated by the bright light and the unfamiliar feel of solid ground under their feet. Only 72 of Neptune's 502 prisoners were able to walk unaided.

Writing in his journal, David Collins said that for some time after the landings the scenes on the west bank of Sydney Cove were 'truly distressing and miserable'

About three dozen tents were set up in front of the temporary hospital to house the sick and the dying. *'Naked, filthy. lousy, wretched, many unable to stand, to creep or even stir hand or foot, were moved from the ships to the improvised hospital.'*

The Reverend Johnson visited all three ships as they were discharging. He saw for himself the dreadful conditions endured by the convicts but even his steadfast dedication to saving souls from damnation would not give him stomach to descend into the stinking holds of Neptune!

In the next few weeks another 150 convicts died, so that of the original number boarding ship in England only two thirds survived and hardly one among these unfortunates was not impaired in some way!

Little in the way of shelter had been prepared for the newcomers who, it had been assumed, would be fit to build their own. Most therefore had to sleep in the open for the immediate future. It was Australia's winter, quite cold, and with only one blanket to cover four men. This contributed to further deaths in the longer term.

The former established residents and old lags of Sydney, who had stood in disbelief as the horror was unfolded before their eyes, were given good cause to recall their own experiences, but remembered nothing to compare with this. If the authorities were beside themselves with rage, Governor Phillip, with his strict views on human values and morality, was driven near apoplectic by the news, especially when it was considered in relation to the colony's own more than satisfactory death rate - only nineteen in the previous twelve months!

The master of the floating charnel house, Neptune, was Captain Donald Traill, a cruel, sadistic man of no conscience whatsoever. Hardly were his tragic charges clear of his ship when he and his first mate opened a shop in Sydney

Village, selling goods which had taken up vital convict space, and the large stock of food gained by starving the convicts. Phillip closed him down, confiscated the food and transferred it into the government store. Letters were then written by the Governor and certain sympathetic marine officers who had been aboard Neptune to witness the crew's inhuman behaviour. These reports, when they reached England, gravely embarrassed the Government which set about a half-hearted tightening of the transportation regulations. By then, however, it was too late to apply them to the Third Fleet which was already on its way, fitted out by the same contractors, under the same terms as the Death Fleet!

It took some time to track down Captain Traill but he was eventually brought to trial in London in 1792. By then, the full impact of his heinous crimes seems to have been blunted in the eyes of the authorities and he was discharged with a mere slap on the wrist!

Also disembarking from the Second Fleet was Captain Nicholas Nepean, at the head of 100 officers and men of the newly (and hastily) constituted New South Wales Regiment. They had come to replace the marines as a permanent, resident garrison and substitute constabulary. Those marines who did not wish to return to England were allowed to transfer to the Regiment.

This was a completely new addition to the British Army and as such possessed none of the long held traditions of discipline and loyalty common in other regiments. Right from the start, its officers showed themselves to be less concerned with military matters and affairs of state than in using their privileges to feather their nests - and feather them well they did! Some of these young wheeler-dealers went on to become the biggest farmers, sheep-rearers and influential merchants in Australia. But that is another story!

In normal circumstances disasters like that of the Second Fleet would have shaken society to its foundations and its repercussions would have lingered until eroded by time. At Sydney Cove, however, society and circumstances were far from normal. This was a nation in embryo, whose every citizen, free or captive, had spent several years staring death in the face. Suffering and deprivation were second nature to the new Australians. When confronted by the obscenity of the Second Fleet, the shock was sharp but very brief to individuals who each considered that their own problems were paramount. When the dead had been laid to rest in the Sandhills, the colonists lapsed back into their self-centred normality.

The badly needed supplies brought by the Fleet were supplemented by the return of Sydney's own ship, Supply, from Batavia. Food rations were increased with variety and nutrition improving. It became possible to issue better clothing; the women were given fabrics and thread with which to make more and nearly everyone obtained a pair of boots.

At the end of 1789, Governor Phillip made land grants to 27 emancipated convicts as an experiment. They were not all successful but by 1790, following the expert example of James Ruse, the colony's only trained farmer, and under the eagle eye of James Dodd, Phillip's free manservant-turned-farmer, there were 200 acres of land cleared and cultivated at Rose Hill. Another 80 acres were enclosed awaiting future cattle imports. Despite a prolonged drought from July 1790 to August 1791, the Rose Hill farms, including Phillip's own, continued to prosper. In November, Rose Hill was given its aborigine name, Parramatta, and Governor Phillip opened up another series of farms at nearby Toongabbie.

At this time, Captain Watkin Tench wrote of Parramatta:-

*'The main street of the new town is begun. It will be a mile long and of such breadth that will make Pall Mall and Portland Place hide their diminished heads. It contains at present 32 houses completed, of 24 feet by 12 each on a ground floor only, built of wattles, plastered with clay and thatched. These houses are designed for men only, 10 to 14 in each with one woman allotted to clean and cook. In a side street are 9 houses for unmarried women.*

*Of public buildings, besides the old wooden barrack, there is the Governor's house of lath and plaster, 44 feet by 16 wide on a ground floor only with excellent outhouses. A new brick storehouse covered with tiles 100 feet long by 24 feet wide ..........*

*In addition, there is an excellent barn, a granary and a commodious blacksmith's shop. A baker is established to bake bread, using the colonists' own flour ration for a stipulated charge.'*

There was also mention of a *'very wretched hospital where sick people were doomed if they should enter it!'*

By this time, the Reverend Richard Johnson had also built a small church and a school for orphan children.

Tench went on to give details of the treatment of convicts at Parramatta:-

*'The hours of labour are the same here as in Sydney. On Saturdays, after 10 in the morning, they are allowed to work in their own gardens, and at the end of every other day if they are so inclined, they can work for anyone else who offers payment for their labour'.*

It was an established fact that this spirit of free enterprise was encouraged among selected, less troublesome convicts as a means towards their eventual removal from reliance on hand-outs from the dwindling food stocks - being 'taken off the store' was the expression used. A number saved their part time wages in order to better themselves when their sentences were served; many of the rest frittered their profits away on drinking, gambling and women; a few used theirs to pay for passage away from Australia.

Whether or not Tench's comments were a fair reflection of the situation, they were in stark contrast to those made by a convict scribe of treatment given at about the same time just down the road at Toongabbie:-

*'They were allowed no breakfast hour for they seldom had anything to eat. From the heat of the sun, the short allowance of provisions and the ill-treatment they received from a set of merciless wretches (most of their own description) who are superintendents, their lives are truly miserable.*

*Some time ago it was not uncommon for seven or eight to die each day, often at work and frequently while being carried to hospital. Many a one died standing in a* queue at the door of the storehouse while waiting for his provision allowance, merely for want of sustenance'.

And another:-

'We were yoked to draw timber in a gang. We held a stake between us six feet long and six men abreast, and dragged with our hands. Only occasionally were we given scraps of food. Each man was expected to clear an acre of ground a week, but the ground was as hard as iron, the timber tough and the few tools we had were useless. We were dreadfully weak from want of food.

I have seen 70 men flogged in a day. Twenty-five lashes each was usual but 300 was not uncommon.'

The reason for this 'other side of the coin 'at Toongabbie was that it had been made the first labour camp for second offenders i.e. convicts who continued to commit crimes in Australia. Conditions for them were deliberately made harsher, although it is doubtful if the Governor went along with the full extent of the barbarity that did exist. He, however, had been placed under pressure from London where reports (mostly magnified) of his leniency were felt to be undermining the deterrent effect of the transportation system.

Thenceforth, Sydney Cove became only the docks and port of access; all attempts at cultivation were abandoned and the many huts and gardens left derelict. The area adjacent to the Tank Stream was a morass where thousands of tramping feet had caved in the dug-out reservoirs along its banks. It was hardly suitable any more for the watering of ships.

The Third Fleet began arriving at Port Jackson in July 1791, and by October the last of the eleven ships was safely at anchor. They were:-

HMS Gorgon, warship, and the ten transports: Active, Admiral Barrington, Atlantic, Albemarle, Britannia, Matilda, Mary Ann, Queen, Salamander and William and Ann.

On setting out, these old, barely seaworthy ships carried 1,869 convicts including 172 women, but en-route one in ten died. The conditions below decks were as bad as ever and in many cases the ships' officers were unspeakably cruel. The really bad apple this time was Queen, carrying the first batch of convicts from Ireland - 148 of them. The brutal captain and first mate kept them all heavily chained in the dark throughout the long voyage and fed them only a quarter of the full ration which in itself was extremely meagre.

Despite the fact that the death toll was only a third that of the Second Fleet, another 171 died soon after landing and a massive 621 were reported as chronically ill!

Also travelling in this fleet were another two companies of the New South Wales Corps under Captain William Paterson whose moment of glory was to come in 1795 when, for a brief nine months, he found himself in sole charge of the colony as deputy Lieutenant Governor.

No more fleets were sent. When word got back to London of the Third Fleet's disgusting record, no public enquiry was held and no blame apportioned, but actions already being taken over the Second Fleet's performance were pursued with greater energy. The contractors were sacked and a revised system of fees brought in. From then on, a price per capita would be paid only for convicts arriving at their destination alive and reasonably well. Between 1792 and 1800, another eighteen ships were to arrive on individual sailings. Some of them were still hell-ships wherein captains took the calculated risk of a larger profit from savings on prisoners' food allowances than in the small bonuses lost by their heartless actions. Gradually, however, much stiffer penalties were introduced for the cruelty of ships' officers, and these awful practices died out.

Not all of the Third Fleet returned to England. Five of its ships were to be seen from time to time at Sydney after their masters chose to go off whaling and sealing in the rich fishing grounds around the forbidding shores of the unexplored Van Diemen's Land.

Governor Phillip was growing very tired. He had been the man at the top for four years, with pressures and responsibilities with which younger, more forceful officers would have struggled to contend, and he had more than coped. By 1792, the burden of anxiety was seen to be taking its toll; he was far from fit, having made the point for so long of subsisting on the same borderline, vitamin-deficient diet as his convicts. His old, aborigine-inflicted spear wound still troubled him and he was in constant pain from a suspected hernia that may have originated in a heavy fall from his horse in the rough country.

His request for retirement went home by way of one of the Third Fleet transports and it was a grudging government that gave its consent.

Towards the end of his governorship there was strong evidence that Phillip was also growing thoroughly disillusioned by the behaviour of the convicts who, for the most part, remained unimproved and totally unrepentant. He was once heard to comment, quite out of character, that 'all murderers, rapists and sodomites in the colony should be put aboard HMS Supply, taken to the wild coast of New Zealand and marooned there to be eaten by cannibals!'

On the 10th December 1792, the transport Atlantic weighed anchor and sailed for home. Standing on her poop deck as she cleared Sydney Heads, Phillip gazed back at his little kingdom for the last time. His thoughts at that moment, though unrecorded, must have been very mixed but, being the man that he was, he would probably have been more aggrieved by his few failures than counting his many achievements!

Here was a man who had been plucked from comparative obscurity by his Government and given the most important task in the world of his day. He had sailed a fleet of eleven small ships over 16,000 miles through notorious seas and delivered them all safely within a day of each other, on the other side of the world. Of his passengers he lost but three per cent!

Given a work force that, through illness and malnutrition, had rarely exceeded five hundred of the most recalcitrant scroungers and layabouts, receiving little co-operation from his military and no support from home, Phillip had apparently accomplished a miracle. Only four and a half years before he had been faced with a densely forested wilderness of iron-hard gum trees, thorn bush, spinifex and giant cabbage trees, infested with poisonous insects and snakes, and populated by unfriendly and often murderous savages. His keen explorations had identified the most promising areas for development along the Parramatta and Hawkesbury Rivers, northwest of Sydney, and these were being taken up as fast as clearance would allow. Here, within two years of his departure, would be found over 400 settlers farming.

Under his direction, a new civilisation had been carved from the most inhospitable of habitats in the corner of the vast southern continent.

Phillip's last, official progress report, on October 12th 1792, demonstrated only too clearly the fruits of his labour.

There were settlements at Sydney Cove, Parramatta, Toongabbie and several other informally named points within a day's march of Port Jackson. The total white population was 3,108 of which 1,948 were convicts and the rest civil department officials, emancipated settlers, children and over 400 military. More than 4,000 convicts had been shipped but the death rolls of the Second and Third Fleets and the subsequent grants of tickets-of-leave had dramatically reduced the number still undergoing sentence. Over 300 time-served men were being allowed to work small pieces of government land for their own upkeep.

Altogether there were 1,700 acres under cultivation, two thirds of them government farms; 1,186 were under maize, 200 under wheat and the rest barley and vegetables. The last crop of maize had made 4,844 bushels although it was later discovered that 1,500 of them had been stolen from the granaries!

These were proud accomplishments - many would say incredible under the circumstances, Arthur Phillip was never without his critics - mostly driven by petty jealousies - but the vast majority of his contemporaries were bound to agree that this dignified and honourable man had at all times ruled his little empire wisely, firmly and justly, tempering his disciplinary measures with carefully calculated mercy. He was well remembered for his nobility, perseverance and little acts of kindness in times of the greatest tribulation.

The exemplary part that he played in the establishment of the young Australian nation is unchallengeable; he was the first, and the most meritorious, of all its governors!

# Chapter 7

## *Postscript*

Arthur Phillip returned home to continue his naval career, rising to the rank of rear admiral in 1801 and to full admiral in 1805, the year of his final retirement. He died in 1814 at the age of 76 having never received the knighthood that many felt he so richly deserved.

The solidly, interlocking foundation blocks of his colonial administration were soon to be seen to be supporting a distinctly unsteady structure that was to stumble from crisis to crisis for the next sixteen years! This was almost totally the result of an absurd form of economy that was introduced accidentally by a militarily orientated, colonial government.

In 1789, 31 year-old Major Francis Grose was sworn in as Lieutenant-Governor of New South Wales, and commissioned to raise the New South Wales Corps for permanent garrison duties in the new colony. He had arrived there himself in 1792 with a second detachment of the regiment and took over command from Captain Paterson. He was then the next senior officer to the governor and there could not have been a greater contrast between the two men, the one being a dignified naval officer and the other an uncouth soldier. Phillip's departure transferred all responsibility to Grose and a series of changes began almost immediately.

Hitherto, the administration was being slowly steered from a naval predominance into a civilian one - still, however, influenced by the lifelong seafaring background of many of its civic dignitaries. With Major Grose at the helm there came a change of direction; the accent was plainly on a military style regime. The colony became a huge barracks with the soldiers eager to take advantage of any concessions that might come from having a Lieutenant-Governor who was also their own commanding officer!

The five civilian magistrates were replaced by officers of the regiment, and others quite happily undertook jury duties. Equality of food rations was ended and the freemen's share increased correspondingly.

The request made by Phillip to London about land grants received assent, but too late for the retiring governor to get the credit for its implementation. Major Grose gleefully commenced a broad interpretation of London's instructions, heavily weighted in favour of his own men.

Officers were awarded 250 acres of land, non-commissioned officers 130 acres and private soldiers 80 acres. An extra 30 acres were given for a wife and 10 acres for each child. Emancipated convicts received 30 acres and any free settlers who might arrive were to be given the same as non-commissioned officers. However, none of the latter stalwart pioneers were seen in the colony until 1793 when the transport Altona sailed in carrying the first ten men, women and children.

The home Government's decree allowed each grantee the services of two convicts to service the farms, but Major Grose turned a blind eye to excesses of this number and he ignored complaints that his officers were poaching the best workers from the government farms. Furthermore, in clear contravention of all military diktats, he did nothing to discourage the taking up of sidelines whereby goods were purchased from passing ships and sold onwards in the colony at huge profits. Unwittingly, therefore, the Major set a pattern that was to alter people's lives irrevocably, creating great wealth for some, ruining others and ultimately leading to a coup d'etat that toppled a governor ( see any history of William Bligh, notorious ex-captain of HMS Bounty and Governor of New South Wales 1806 to 1808).

Any other hand on the tiller but that of Major Grose might have taken Australian history in an entirely different direction!

Early in 1793, an American trader, 'Hope', arrived in Sydney laden with nails, flour, cloth and 7,500 gallons of rum. Shortly afterwards, another American, 'Philadelphia', sailed in loaded with barrels of cured beef, gin, rum and wine.

The shrewd, hard-bargaining captains of these ships wanted quick turn-rounds, no doubt in order to set off for the teeming whaling grounds to fill their holds with skins which would make their journeys back to America as lucrative as the outward one! They refused to sell their cargoes piecemeal but demanded to trade them whole as single lots or not at all. This proved no obstacle to the army officers who were in a privileged position through the clever accountancy of their paymaster, Lieutenant Macarthur, to raise sufficient funds against IOUs and promissory notes on their salaries. Pooling this money, they formed a monopolistic syndicate to purchase both cargoes. These were then traded throughout the colony at profits of up to 1,000 per cent!

And so it went on. By the end of 1793 ships were turning up from England, India, America, Batavia and China, discharging all manner of goods, both practical and luxury - but chiefly rum for which demand was always the greatest.

The fiery spirits that varied in flavour from vile, through several stages of indifferent, to sometime excellence, all passed under the same name 'rum', and its consumption in great quantities, offered one sure avenue of temporary relief from the boredom and wretchedness felt in every level of class throughout the colony. Anything could be obtained for rum: for a barrel, the building of a small house or the acquisition of a farm acreage!

In a land where coinage had yet to be introduced, and where no bank existed, rum became the currency and the military the bankers who controlled its supply. While rum was king, the 102nd Regiment, New South Wales Corps was more commonly referred to as 'The Rum Regiment' and its officers were the rum barons who formed themselves into a snobbish, elite clique, holding a tight monopoly on all trade in the colony.

Judge-Advocate David Collins, writing in 1793, had this to say:-

'At Sydney and Parramatta, shops were opened for the sale of articles brought out by 'The Royal Admiral'. A licence was given for the sale of porter but, under cover of this, spirits found their way among the people and much intoxication was the consequence. Several of the settlers, breaking out of the restraint to which they had been subject, conducted themselves with the greatest impropriety, beating their wives, destroying their stock, trampling on and injuring the crops in the ground and destroying each other's property'.

Two years later he was writing:-

'The passion for liquor is so predominant among the people that it acts like a mania, there being nothing that they would not risk to obtain it, and while spirits are to be had, those who do any extra labour refuse to be paid in money or any other article than spirits which are now, for their scarcity, sold at six shillings a bottle!'

A settler named Webb, who lived near Parramatta, having procured a small still from England, found it was more advantageous to draw the notorious spirit from his wheat than to send it to the store and receive ten shillings a bushel for it! From one bushel of wheat he obtained nearly five quarts of spirit which he sold or paid in exchange for labour at five or six shillings a quart!

Rum bought from ships for eight shillings a gallon could easily be resold at eight pounds a gallon!

This was the craving that the military set out to exploit and over the next four years they nearly succeeded in turning Australia into a nation of alcoholics. With their rapidly amassing wealth they even began to charter ships of their own to go abroad in search of lucrative cargoes. Before long the Rum Corps owned the bulk of all the livestock and a large proportion of all the land in and around Sydney!

Much of the grain grown on this land was used to make rum with which the military estates were built up by the purchase of more farms from ex-convicts and free settlers who became ruined by their weakness for drink. The power of the Regiment was all-embracing. The colony became a breeding ground for opportunists, and a graveyard for their victims; the soldiers began to act as badly as the felons they were guarding. As this new, elitist class gathered way, it swaggered, postured and vaunted its superiority in all manner of ways, one of the worst being an escalation of extreme cruelty and brutality towards the convicts and any free settlers who might have given offence!

It was chiefly due to this rum-subsidised society that the convicts and their families remained in a sort of purgatory for many years to come. Those who had served their sentences joined the ranks of the 'emancipists', a class from which they were not allowed to escape, no matter how fortune treated them in the future. Their criminal records, even if only lightly earned, ensured that neither they nor several generations of their families would be granted the status enjoyed by the 'exclusives', the rich farmers and merchants whose forbears had come to Australia of their own free will.

Of the latter, probably the most notable was a man who arrived with the Second Fleet, with the first contingent of the New South Wales Corps. Lieutenant John Macarthur became paymaster to the Regiment and thereafter master-minded the financial and business affairs of his brother officers.

He and his very resourceful wife, Elizabeth, were granted their 280 acres of land next to the successful farm of James Ruse at Parramatta. This became known as Elizabeth Farm, and in the space of only three years up until 1795, had 100 acres under cultivation and the rest cleared in readiness for furrowing by the first plough to be seen in the colony!

By this time, the Macarthurs had 1,000 bushels of wheat and 1,800 bushels of corn in their granaries, 2 mares, 2 cows, 130 goats, over 100 hogs and abundant poultry. On the farm they lived in a strong, brick house of one storey, measuring 18 feet by 68 feet, with a three acre garden full of vines, fruit trees and vegetables. Nearby, and very convenient for Lieutenant Macarthur's official duties, was a newly-built barracks.

But his main interest was in sheep and the production of quality wool.

In 1794, Macarthur imported 60 Bengal ewes and lambs. Shortly afterwards he got hold of 20 South African merinos. Two years later he bought 1,200 sheep of the common Cape breed from Major Foveaux who was about to transfer to Norfolk Island to commence his infamous reign of terror.

At the time, this made Macarthur the largest sheep owner in New South Wales, bearing in mind that this was then the only state, comprising almost half the continent. By careful and astute cross-breeding, he obtained a hardy strain of merino, very much at home in the Australian climate and bearing a fleece of the softest, highest quality texture seen anywhere in the world up to that time.

Then his luck seemed to desert him. In 1801, his volatile nature caused a falling-out with his commanding officer, Lieutenant Colonel Paterson, whom he wounded superficially in a duel. For his court martial, Governor Gidley King, sent Macarthur to London in order to obtain the impartiality that would be absent from a court made up of brother officers. More than anything else, King wanted to rid himself of this pestilential ringleader of the notorious Rum Corps, who for years had bedevilled the colony's governors. However, the plan misfired when the London court acquitted Macarthur. He had gone to England well prepared!

Through contacts and cronies in London he found his way into influential circles where he demonstrated woollen samples of the results of his interbreeding experiments. The Privy Council was most impressed and eventually the Colonial Office sent Macarthur back to Australia with instructions for Governor King to award him 10,000 acres on which to build up his flocks of top quality, wool-bearing merinos. He was also given thirty convicts as his labour force. With him from England in 1805, he brought another seven merino rams and three ewes which someone had inadvertently (and illegally) allowed him to buy from the private stud of King George at Kew!

The land that Macarthur finally settled upon was in an area about forty miles from Sydney named Cowpastures in honour of over 700 wild cattle found living there - the progeny of the few domestic bulls and cows that had wandered off in the early days of Sydney Cove and which had been providentially spared by aborigine hunters. The Macarthurs renamed the place Camden after the 2nd Earl of Camden who, as Colonial Secretary, had sanctioned the land grant and made their fortunes by creating the circumstances which enabled them to become the most successful sheep breeders in New South Wales on stations that ultimately exceeded 60,000 acres! This was not bad for a couple who had originally left England with debts of £500. But they were not the only ones by far!

The Reverend Samuel Marsden, who replaced Richard Johnson as colony chaplain, went from saver of souls to being the most severe of magistrates, earning for himself the name 'The Flogging Parson', hating convicts, dishing out sentences of up to 500 lashes and making full use of his judicial powers to profit from the ruination of his human flock. For a while, his expertise as a sheep farmer and his 6,000 acres of good grazing land were second only to that of John Macarthur. But it was not only the freeborn settlers who made their fortunes!

A mere eight tears after his transportation for theft in 1790, emancipated Simeon Lloyd began investment in shipping, whaling and the salt pork trade with the Pacific islands. By 1803 he lived in an opulent mansion in Sydney!

Henry Kable arrived with the First Fleet after his death sentence for burglary was commuted to 14 years transportation. Following success in the rum trade, he joined partnership with James Underwood, convicted for stealing but a skilful boat-builder. Between them they had fingers dipped in rich pies consisting of shipping, whaling and manufacturing.

Samuel Terry was a thief who received seven years transportation. He became a tavern keeper and moneylender, in which capacities he was able to bankrupt many of his customers through drink and debt so that their smallholdings and livestock came into his possession by default. Before his fiftieth birthday he owned 20,000 acres!

There were many others!

What ex-Governor Arthur Phillip might have thought of these deviations from his forthright policies is anybody's guess. Certainly they were not his ways, and even more certainly, if he had not retired when he did, the rum trade would not have been allowed to get so out of hand. That it did was down to the weakness and irresolution of succeeding governors up until 1810 when Lachlan Macquarie broke the vicious stranglehold and obtained the recall of the Rum Corps to England.

In all probability, Phillip would not have approved wholeheartedly of the respectable elevation that some of the convicts achieved. He had never agreed completely with the Home Government's judgement that transportation should be a punishment and a deterrent continuing long after a sentence was completed. He did believe in giving those who had paid their debts to society, a chance to become small farmers and earn their own livings. However, it is hardly likely that he would have commended the idea of common criminals being ultimately rewarded by admittance to the ranks of the wealthiest freemen.

Nevertheless, this was how the destiny of Australia was shaped - laboriously but honestly at first, capriciously and greedily later - with the penal system always pumping life-blood in the form of cheap labour, until the last convict transport ship sailed into Freemantle in 1868!

# *Bibliography*

History of Australia                                                     Marjorie Barnard

Australia – The Creation of a Nation  1788-1988            Charles Wilson

The Story of Australia                                                  A. G. L. Shaw

A History of Australia                                                  C. M. H. Clark

Concise Oxford Dictionary of Australian History            Jan Basset

Mastering Australian History                                      Ronald Laidlaw

A Short History of Australia                                        Manning Clark

Beyond the Black Stump
-Tales of Travellers to Australia 1787 to 1850              Michael Foss

The First Fleet                                                          Jonathan King

Australia and the Australians                                      R. M. Younger

Australians from Wales                                              Lewis Lloyd

Encyclopaedia of Australia                  A, T. A. & A. M. Learmouth

The Fatal Shore                                                        Robert Hughes

The National Library of Australia Canberra

The State Library of New South Wales Sydney

The National History Museum London